THE
RIVER CONWY
Source to Sea

with the rivers
Machno, Lledr and Llugwy

Photography
JEAN NAPIER

Text
ALUN JOHN RICHARDS

First published: 2011

Cover Design: Jean Napier
© Photography: Jean Napier   Text: Alun John Richards

ISBN: 978-1-84527-288-3

Published by
Gwasg Carreg Gwalch,
12 Iard yr Orsaf, Llanrwst, Wales, LL26 0EH.
Tel: 01492 642031 Fax: 01492 641502
e-mail: llyfrau@carreg-gwalch.co.uk
www.carreg-gwalch.co.uk

Printed and published in Wales

Jean Napier ARPS

Jean has lived in the Snowdonia National Park since 1991 and the magnificent variety of scenery within the Park is her main inspiration. Man's archaeological and industrial influences on the landscape are a recurring theme in her exhibitions and books.

Her primary motivation is to promote photography as an art form; to explore how the camera can be used as a creative tool not just as a means for recording moments. Her work has been exhibited throughout the UK, the USA and Australia.

She runs photography workshops with students of all ages and abilities. Jean holds a BA Honours Degree in Photographic Studies and is an Associate of the Royal Photographic Society. *www.jean-napier.com*

Alun John Richards

Retired engineer, ex-professional pilot, sometime motorcycle instructor of instructors, Swansea born and based, Alun suffered singularly un-academic sojourns at Bishop Gore Grammar School and University College Swansea.

A native of Swansea he is a past Chairman of the South West Wales Industrial Archaeology Society and of the Swansea Art Society and President of South Wales Advanced Motorcyclists.

He was for many years a Guest Field Lecturer at the Snowdonia National Park Environmental Studies Centre, Plas Tan y Bwlch, specialising in the Welsh slate industry and was an occasional lecturer at Coleg Harlech Summer Schools. *www.richards-slate.co.uk*

Cati

A crossbreed border collie/lurcher, Cati has been Jean's faithful photography assistant for over 9 years accompanying Jean on endless adventures throughout the Welsh landscape – Cati indulging in her passion for chasing squirrels and rabbits.

Foreword

From source to sea, Afon Conwy flows through a series of some of Wales' most dramatic landscapes. Rising from Llyn Conwy, on the vast moorlands of the Migneint echoing to the calls of curlew and red grouse, it flows briefly eastwards before turning sharply north and plummeting down a series of moss-encrusted gorges towards Betws-y-coed, then leisurely snaking its way past Llanrwst and on towards the estuary and the town of Conwy itself.

The river connects the Knights of St John with the Romans, Bishop William Morgan with Thomas Telford and ancient plagues with modern disaster. It has seen enough wars, invasions and tragedy to put all other Welsh rivers to shame and yet it remains a peaceful and tranquil watercourse, a place for wildlife and people to enjoy.

Nowhere has the history of this magnificent river been told so comprehensively as in this book. Alun Richards' words bring that history to life and Jean Napier's stunning photography ensures that the sounds of the cascading water ring in your ears as you read in the comfort of your own home. This book, the third in the series, is a must have for anyone with a thirst for knowledge and a love of history and the countryside.

Iolo Williams

Introduction

The Conwy is, apart from the Tywi, the longest and largest river that flows entirely within Wales. The Severn, that the Romans romantically called *Sabrina*, took England as a husband, the Dee struggled to hold its Welsh identity, but ultimately could only find the sea by English espousal. The Wye has one bank in England, but a frontier function can scarcely be held to be a disadvantage since the Conwy had a similar role in defending the lairs of the Ordoviciae from the onslaughts of the Decaengli. The Romans established enclaves within the Conwy's ambit but only ventured outside their palisades mob-handed. The Normans established sea-supplied castles at Caernarfon, Harlech and to the west of Conwy's estuary but generally only travelled beyond the Conwy with trepidation and circumspection. Even in the 18th century when travel to Ireland became popular, forsaking the rural respectability of Denbighshire for the cutpurse territory of Caernarfonshire must have been dreaded.

Besides its erstwhile military function, this river is a geological and economic frontier. To the east is a land of villages, agriculture and rolling moorland. To the west is a hard, unforgiving landscape of mineral-rich rock with lakes, waterfalls and intensive coniferous forestation that leads to some of the most desolate and deserted land in Britain.

This age-old bisection lives on as an administrative separation and is still aurally detectable. Those keen of ear can distinguish a native of Conwy town from one of Deganwy and, even some claim, differentiate the accents of Llanrwst from those of Trefriw.

The lower Conwy was navigable affording sea-going vessels an approach to the northern Welsh heartlands, and it was the only Welsh river to support a pleasure steamship service.

*Dedicated to all those kind people who welcomed us onto their land,
into their homes and shared reminiscence, fact and fable,
and so made this book possible*

Previous Books

JEAN NAPIER with ALUN JOHN RICHARDS
A Tale of Two Rivers   ISBN 978-0-86381-989-6
Two Snowdonia Rivers   ISBN 978-1-84527-206-7

JEAN NAPIER
Rhosydd A Personal View − Golwg Bersonol   ISBN 978-0-86381-470-9

ALUN JOHN RICHARDS
A Gazeteer of the Welsh Slate Industry   ISBN 978-0-86381-196-5
Slate Quarrying at Corris   ISBN 978-0-86381-279-1
Slate Quarrying in Wales   ISBN 978-0-86381-319-4
Slate Quarrying in Pembrokeshire   ISBN 978-0-86381-484-0
The Slate Regions of North& Mid Wales   ISBN 978-0-86381-552-9
The Slate Railways of Wales   ISBN 978-0-86381-689-5
Fragments of Mine and Mill   ISBN 978-0-86381-812-7
Cwm Gwyrfai (with Gwynfor Pierce Jones)   ISBN 978-0-86381-897-4
Welsh Slate Craft   ISBN 978-1-84527-029-2
Crefftwyr Llechi   ISBN 978-1-84527-034-6
Slate Quarrying in Wales (Revised)   ISBN 978-1-84527-026-1
Published by Gwasg Carreg Gwalch, Llanrwst, Wales

Gazeteer of Slate Quarrying in Wales   ISBN 978-1-84524-074-5
Slate Quarrying in Corris   ISBN 978-1-84524-068-5
Tinplate in Wales   ISBN 978-1-84524-125-4
Rails & Sails of Welsh Slate   ISBN 978-1-84524-174-2
Published by Llygad Gwalch, Llwyndyrys, Wales

Contents

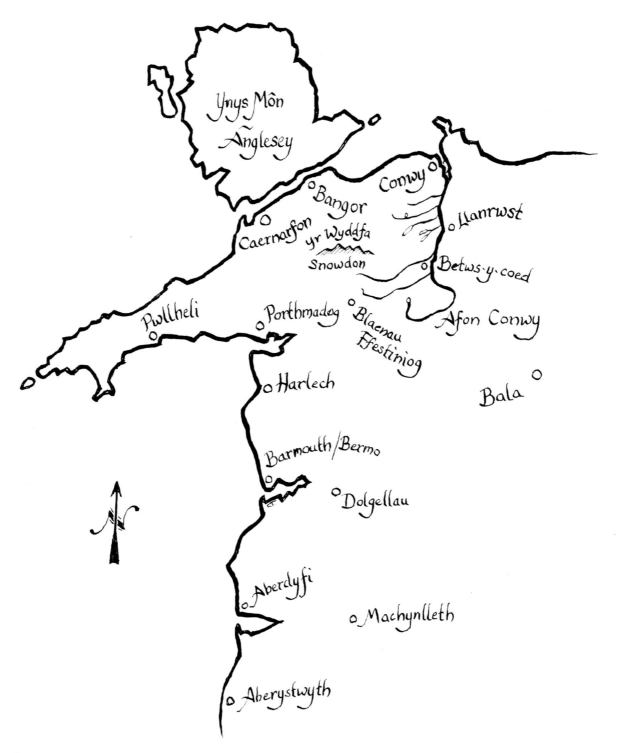

Ynys Môn
Ãnglesey

Conwy

Bangor

Caernarfon

yr Wyddfa

Snowdon

Llanrwst

Betws-y-coed

Pwllheli

Porthmadog

Blaenau
Ffestiniog

Afon Conwy

Harlech

Bala

Barmouth/Bermo

Dolgellau

Aberdyfi

Machynlleth

Aberystwyth

N

Words from Gruff Ellis

I feel privileged to add a few words to this book on a river that has since childhood, always been an important part of my life. I was born about 50 yards from its bank and still live as near as ever today. Alun's prose and Jean's amazing photography touch me deeply.

From its source on the Migneint it flows among the heather and cotton grass, the red grouse and the golden plover down through the rugged gorges, until it meets the estuary at Glan Conwy.

I've sat on its banks for hours watching grey wagtails flit from rock to rock, the dipper busy as ever diving for morsels for its nestlings, or sometimes the long legged heron standing patiently waiting for a minnow to satisfy its hunger.

The Conwy from Llyn Conwy to the bridge at Rhydlanfair and beyond is my 'soul mate' when I am fishing or meditating on its banks or on its familiar tributaries.

I have been moved by its tranquillity in spring and summer and its raging torrents in autumn and winter; Jean and Alun have put this all together in their book.

Thank you Jean and Alun for the opportunity of sharing with you my beloved Conwy.

Gruff Ellis
Ysbyty Ifan

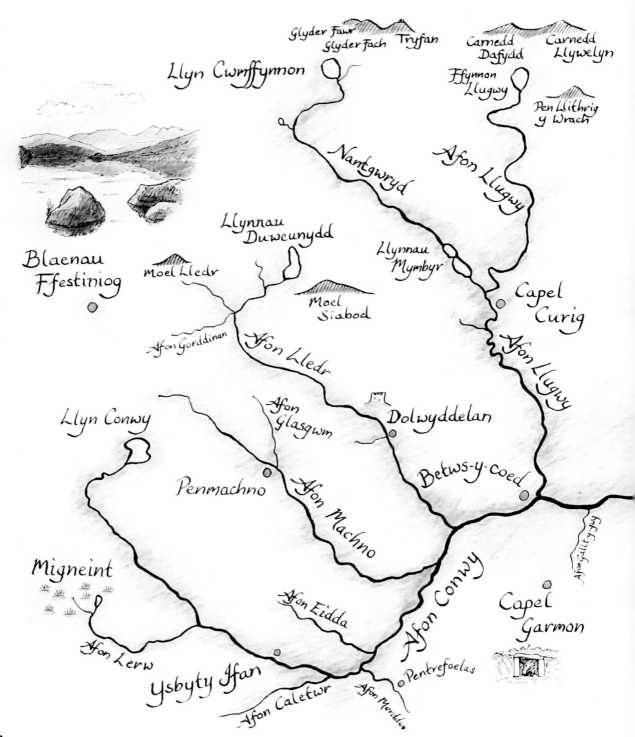

Glyder Fawr
Glyder Fach   Tryfan
Carnedd
Dafydd   Carnedd
Llywelyn

Llyn Cwmffynnon

Ffynnon
Llugwy

Pen Llithrig
y Wrach

Nantgwryd

Afon Llugwy

Llynnau
Duweunydd

Llynnau
Mymbyr

Moel Lledr

Capel
Curig

Blaenau
Ffestiniog

Moel
Siabod

Afon Gorddinan

Afon Lledr

Afon Llugwy

Llyn Conwy

Afon
Glasgwm

Dolwyddelan

Penmachno

Betws-y-coed

Afon Machno

Afon Gallt-y-Hy

Migneint

Capel
Garmon

Afon Eidda

Afon Conwy

Afon Lerw

Pentrefoelas

Ysbyty Ifan

Afon Caletwr   Afon Merddwr

Llanfairfechan

Melynllyn
Llyn Dulyn
Llyn Eigiau
Penmaenmawr
Afon Porth-llwyd
Afon Dulyn
Conwy
Llyn Cowlyd
Afon Ddu
Tal-y-bont
Deganwy
Llandudno
Llyn Crafnant
Dolgarrog
Glan Conwy
Llyn Geirionydd
Bodnant
Afon Crafnant
Trefriw
Afon Conwy
Llanrwst

Afon Conwy

1
THE SOURCE

Many rivers just seem to happen – springs wet the ground, rivulets mingle to form a nascent stream, rendering it impossible to precisely identify the source. In the case of the Conwy there is no debate, the source is indisputably Llyn Conwy. Although Llyn Conwy is a pigmy besides the thousand acres of Tegid (Bala) or Trawsfynydd, at a hundred acres it just qualifies for the 'Ton-up club'. Whether in summer's sun or winter's cruellest chill it is a place of tranquil peace.

Allegedly it was once owned by the Knights of St John of Jerusalem of Ysbyty Ifan to ensure a supply of fresh fish for their Friday lunches. True or not, what is fact is that it was owned in more recent times by an almost equally grandiose organisation – the Penrhyn Estate.

The Lords Penrhyn were not noted for their generosity towards their workers or their tenants but they were expansive hosts and their shooting and fishing parties at Llyn Conwy were legendary. Being some distance from their Capel Curig Hotel (now Plas-y-Brenin) and even further from

Penrhyn Castle itself, a trip to the Migneint was a sleepover job. Hence the still surviving Llyn Cottage near the road and the now ruined lodge near the lake to accommodate the sportsmen. Well-stocked and nurtured, trout abounded as did poachers, so in the latter part of the 19th century it became virtually an armed camp whose defenders were more commandos than bailiffs. To ensure that there were no relatives or friends to favour, English and Scottish hard men were imported from afar but they were no match for the wily Welsh poachers. They had more success guarding the grouse which with predatory birds ruthlessly eliminated, thrived in their thousands to be slaughtered on an industrial scale at the nearby Nant y Groes Butts.

Later dammed to provide a public water supply, the lake has traces of what seems to have been a hatchery. A tiny island (George Borrow mentions there being three) is an aircraft carrier for black-backed gulls. During the 20th century, neglect and acidity caused the fish population to taper off, but lime release has reduced its acidity and the fish-pass at Betws-y-coed will undoubtedly bring some regeneration and provide better sport for the fly-fishing club. According to local lore, there are six springs rising underneath the lake. It is a fact however that its water level is hardly affected by severe summer droughts and it seldoms freezes over in winters.

Remote and isolated, the infant river seems to have pondered which way to escape the lake. It could well have gone south to throw in its lot with the Dee and debouch into Liverpool Bay. It could have gone west to augment the collection of streams that unite as the Dwyryd to reach Cardigan Bay. In the event it went north, but shunning the obviousness of Cwm Machno, feinted towards the south before swinging in a mighty curve to plough an independent furrow.

With the help of the waters of the Groes, the Ddu, the Las, the Llwyni Hywel and the rather more substantial Serw, quite a respectable stream sets about defining the Conwy Valley proper, tumbling its way to Ysbyty Ifan where the hills create a mini climate with lush pasture that contrasts with the bleak moorland. Having passed under its first bridge the Pont ar Gonwy shortly after escaping from Llyn Conwy, (that although rebuilt, it retains its original clapper-bridge profile), it is not crossed again until Ysbyty Ifan where a nice arch was built during the late 18th century, later replaced by the present unremarkable structure.

Ysbyty Ifan was a settlement dedicated to serving the preceptory of the Knights of St John of Jerusalem, its name literally meaning the hospital of Ifan (*Evan*). The term hospital traditionally meaning a place of Sanctuary where both the hale and the sick could find hospitality, this one being founded here at what was then Dôl Gynwal by Ifan ap Rhys of Plas Iolyn, Pentrefoelas in the late 12th century to provide sanctuary for travellers from bandits and others of a rapacious disposition who lurked hereabouts with felonious intent. Damaged by Edward I, burnt during the independence war of Owain Glyndŵr, by the late 15th century the hospice had become

almost a den of thieves. Since temporal authority was not recognised within its bounds, it could shelter those very villains that it was supposed to exclude, making it a secure base for organised crime. This immunity was aided by the river being the boundary between Denbighshire and Meirionnydd, thus any wrongdoer being pursued by his county's constables had only a brief wade to place himself beyond their reach.

Henry VII constrained some of such anomalies and Henry VIII finally put a stop to the whole concept of Sanctuary by dissolving the Order and devolving some its privileges to the Lords of the Manor. All trace of the hospital was eradicated by building a church on its site. This had a chapel on either side, one for the Foelas family and the other for the rival Pant Glas family so that both could worship without actually meeting. By the 1840s a school had been established to the rear. The school received a less than flattering write-up in the Parliamentary Report on Education in Wales –

"The school is held in a part of the parish church, separated by a partition for the purpose. It was very dirty and ill ventilated. The furniture consists of a few old benches taken out of the church, and one small desk; they are

insufficient for the purpose, and were filthy with smoke. The master has been engaged in teaching for 26 years, but was never trained for the purpose. He could speak very few words of English; he was living in a miserable cottage, and appeared dirty and very poor."

This building was replaced by the present church of St John the Baptist in 1861 that contains alabaster effigies of 'Rhys Fawr' (Rhys ap Maredudd) and his wife, Lowri. Maredudd's pivotal contribution to Henry VII's victory at Bosworth earned him the vast Rhiwlas estate. His grandson became chaplain to Cardinal Wolsey and a key figure in the Reformation. A later descendent was R.J.L. (Squire) Price, pioneer of sheep dog trials and distiller of Frongoch whisky. A plaque and a stained glass window testify to the continued interest in the in the church by the Order of St John and the Hospitalers' Club of Wales.

The Reformation effectively converted all the parish churches in England and Wales to the Anglican persuasion, but there were many people who wanted more radical reform. The first of these 'dissenters' to make an impact were the Baptists of the 17th century followed in the 18th century by Calvin and Wesley, scornfully called 'Methodists'. Such was the influence of Calvin in Wales that by the mid 19th century more than half of all places of worship in Wales were Calvinistic Methodist (Presbyterian), as is the early chapel at Ysbyty Ifan. During the latter 19th century when a fresh chapel was opening every eight days, the new establishments tended to be Independent (*Annibynnwr*), making this Congregational

denomination increasingly the chapel of choice. Thus a pre mid-19th century chapel is likely to be Calvinistic, post mid 19th century the odds are that it will be Congregational.

As a subsidiary industry Ysbyty Ifan had two wells, neither on the scale of the great spas, but were what we would now call 'Visitor Attractions', the vile taste of their waters testifying to their efficacy. Such wells often provided some semblance of sustenance for elderly widows, who could sit by them and sell 'cures'. A highly dangerous occupation since if the cure failed the late patient's relatives might seek vengeance while a successful cure could well be held to be satanically inspired thus identifying the hapless crone as a witch, meriting instant immolation.

Almost all riverside villages had a flour mill, most have fallen into ruin, but after a spell as an hydro generating station the Ysbyty Ifan mill has its wheel and much of its machinery preserved intact and finds a new use as a village-based wedding supplies business.

An industry of wider importance was droving. During the 18th & 19th centuries increasing urbanisation called for foodstuffs to be moved from the countryside to London and other fast-growing towns and cities in ever-increasing quantities. With transport expensive and uncertain, this food had to be 'self-propelled'; hence cattle, sheep and sometimes poultry from Wales and even

Ireland were driven across country. This upper Conwy valley was a droving route, Ffynnon Eidda, the drovers' well and the site of a long-vanished inn on the Migneint where the Penmachno road leaves the Ysbyty Ifan road being a relic of this.

The drovers' contribution to the invention of banking is often exaggerated and romanticised, they did handle large sums of money and enjoyed a certain respect but defalcations were not unknown. Although most were men of standing, some were not and their arrival in a village was not necessarily good news. However the hiring of fields to overnight the beasts, the shoeing of cattle and the feeding and watering of both drovers and animals offered profitable opportunities to places *en route*.

Augmented by Afon Caletwr, the river makes its first major alliance, with the Merddwr near Penrefoelas and alongside the hustle and bustle of Thomas Telford's Great Irish Road, absorbs the Nant y Coed and Afon Gwrysgog from the north and Afon Eidda and Nant Fforchog from the south, close to where Hen Foelas Motte dominates the valley.

Thomas Telford's road, the most ambitious road-building project since Roman times, was very much a strategic enterprise partly aimed at tying London and Dublin closer together following the Act of Union of Ireland in 1800 and partly to keep the Irish on side since they were suspected of being sympathetic to Napoleon. Travellers could board the Irish packet at Holyhead a mere 27 hours after leaving Marble Arch.

To maintain this almost 10 mph average, horses were changed at an inn every 10 miles or so, horn-blasts from the guard of the approaching coach having ensured that ostlers were standing by with harnessed horses so the incoming four could be replaced with a dispatch that would not disgrace a Formula 1 pit-crew changing wheels. Meal stops at places such as Betws-y-coed would be long enough to eat or attend to a call of nature, but possibly not both, posing a challenging dilemma. Coaching inns were notorious for their uneatable and overpriced food, in some cases taking so long to serve it that passengers, despite having paid in advance, had no time to eat it – thus enabling the same portions to be warmed up for the next arrivals!

Curiously, although the stage and mail coaches thanks to Charles Dickens and a zillion Christmas cards have come to epitomise Ye Olde England, the heyday of coaching lasted scarcely four decades before being overtaken by the railways. The Holyhead coach was finally eclipsed by the opening of the Britannia railway bridge in 1849.

A side road crosses the river via Pont Rhydydyfrgi, which is a span built in 1788 by Charles Finch, to ensure that the boots of the hoi polloi did not soil the access bridge to Foelas House. Finch, the slightly impoverished second son of the then Earl of Aylesford, had ten years earlier the good

sense to marry Jane Wynn the sole heiress to the Foelas estate and owner in her own right of estates on Anglesey. Apart from acquiring a substantial fortune and stylish place to hang his hat, Finch also acquired entry into one of the leading families of Wales, who claimed kinship with Rhys ap Maredudd. Finch's son built the present church at Pentrefoelas and his grandson built the present Foelas house. Jane Wynn's sister escaped the

impecuniousness of a younger sibling by marrying into the Assheton-Smith family of the Faenol Estate, so furthering the Finch-Wynn's influence.

Just beyond at the notorious Padog bends the road crosses to the south of the river by Telford's Padog Bridge. A little further on a side road is carried across the Conwy by Pont Rhydlanfair, a magnificent 90' span and arguably the best bridge on the upper rivers. Now reinforced by the Machno, the Conwy takes on board Afon Eidda and Nant Fforchog and goes down the spectacular Rhaeadr y Graig Lwyd cascade. The falls have lost some of their water to the tunnelled fish pass that enable Atlantic salmon to find spawning grounds in the highest reaches of the river system. Emerging from the fall's cauldron, the river plunges into the depths of the smoulderingly dank gorge of Ffos Noddyn, once considered to be the entrance to Annwn, the Welsh fairy underworld of mysterious happenings –

now touristically tagged 'Fairy Glen'. The river now makes union with Afon Lledr at Llyn yr Afanc ('*beaver pool*') where it is watched over with disinterested distain by the Zwartbles sheep of Cwmanog Isaf.

There is confusion as to the origin of the name Llyn yr Afanc. Was it once the haunt of beavers or something more sinister – the *afanc*, that dreadful monster that shares is name in Welsh with the cuddly, dam-building little creatures? The legend of Llyn Diwaunydd has its *afanc* originating here so does the name refer to the beast or to the beavers that could certainly have lived here up to around the 11th century? It is possible that a few generations-worth of exaggeration has expanded these cat-sized animals into monsters of fearsome proportions. The road from Dolwyddelan runs past the vestiges of a tollhouse, originally reaching Betws by continuing straight on but the modern road jinks right over the Pont Llyn yr Afanc to join the A5.

Reaching down to the river here are the tree-enriched gardens of Coed y Celyn Hall, a magnificent wrought-iron gated manor house. Although much has been modernised into apartments some rooms retain their awesome splendour of Wedgwood decor and a Carrera marble fireplace.

2
MACHNO

Closely paralleling the upper Conwy and joining with it near Bont Newydd is Afon Machno. Its valley, longer and more populous than the upper Conwy, reputedly has nurtured more Ministers of Religion per 100 population than anywhere else on earth. As soon as it has gathered a clutch of streamlets, including the quaintly named Nant Beti Richards and emerged from its Twll-y-cwm birthplace, it confronts the one-industry (but sadly now non-industry) village of Cwm Penmachno.

Nucleated around the Cwm Machno slate quarry, this village of quarry-owned houses was despite a population of a mere 400, virtually self-contained. There were a dozen shops selling food, clothes and day-to-day necessities, including a butcher with his own abattoir, and of course a Co-op selling almost everything. Peddlers would make periodic visits selling amongst other things a surprising number of books. The resident coal merchant brought in fuel from Betws-y-coed, and a baker could either sell you a loaf for a penny or bake your own quartern for a farthing and there

was a shoemaker who actually made shoes rather than being just a 'soler & heeler'. A carpenter made furniture and the quarry blacksmith could re-tyre a cartwheel, make a chisel or forge almost anything. There was a school and a pair of pubs, a chapel and in the 20th century a garage repairing cars and selling petrol. There was a Post Office, an amenity now sadly lacking in so many communities. Curiously, the postman having collected the mail from Betws-y-coed sorting office at the crack of dawn, cycled out to Cwm Penmachno to deliver house-to-house, then spent the day sitting in a little hut waiting to empty the post box at 3.00 pm.

There were a numerous societies in Cwm Penmachno but outstripping even the choirs, the football team and the *Urdd Gobaith Cymru* (Welsh Guild of Youth) as a focus of village pride and joy, was The Band which had its own practice hut.

Joining the Machno at the village is Nant Drum Boeth, literally 'stream of the hot ridge', the name suggest's that it faces the summer sun. It is certainly a multi-purpose water-course, having driven the water-wheels of Rhiwbach slate quarry and served as a water supply (and sewer!) to the Rhiwbach quarry settlement, it was impounded to serve the wheels and turbines of Cwm Machno slate quarry which was the hub of several subsidiary workings. Besides powering the mills and air compressors, it drove one of the finest water balance inclines in the industry, which was used to raise material within the quarry. Actually there were at one time plans to create

a truly mighty water balance to take the output up to the Rhiwbach Tramway and thence to Blaenau Ffestiniog, rather than cart it down the valley. Yet despite being handicapped by having to cart all output to Betws-y-coed (and earlier to Trefriw), Cwm Machno quarry outlasted most of its competitors only closing in 1962 due to a shortage of skilled men. The quarry used one of the very first steam lorries but an uncertainty of brakes and steering coupled with a 'learn as you go' attitude towards driving skills, led to accidents and it at least once ended in Afon Machno.

Actually Cwm Penmachno might well have found itself rail connected; when the London & North Western Railway's line to Blaenau Ffestiniog became stalled at Betws-y-coed due to the problems of boring through the diamond-hard rock of Moel Dwynogydd at the head of the Lledr valley, there was a slightly madcap scheme to run the line up the Machno valley and tunnel through to Blaenau from Cwm Penmachno. There were also at one time plans for a railway from Corwen to Betws-y-coed that would have had a branch up the Machno valley. Such developments besides putting the Machno valley on the map would have helped Cerrigydrudion to maintain the importance that Telford's road had brought it and which vanished with the coming of the railways.

Although much of the upper part of Cwm Machno quarry continues to defy time, weather and vandalism, the lower part has been blandly landscaped, obliterating the fine crenulated boundary wall, which carried a rubbish track, and the portico that would have been worthy of a Norman castle. To the north of the village is the opening to a most curious tunnel. This is Glyn Aber that drained the underground workings at Rhiwbach quarry and provided some outlet for spoil. Had Cwm Penmachno found itself railway-served, this tunnel might have become an outlet for Rhiwbach's finished product.

Having been joined near Cwm Penmachno by Nant Dyfnant and Nant y Foel, the latter crashing down Cwm Hafodyredwydd alongside the road from Ffynnon Eidda; a couple of miles down valley the Machno is further augmented by the Oernant. Its name *Cold Brook* is well chosen, cascading as it does from the icy heights of the Migneint, quite close to Llyn Conwy.

Half a mile down-valley is Penmachno, the 'Capital' of the valley and a traditional intersection of routes. To the southeast the road is now a dead-end, but once was a route to Ysbyty Ifan and to the west the road reaches up towards Blaen Glasgwm, once a route to Dolwyddelan. The sole cross route surviving as a vehicle thoroughfare branches north from this Glasgwm road to reach the Lledr valley. Although providing a somewhat adventurous journey, it is much travelled since it passes Ty'n y Coed Uchaf a preserved traditional Welsh farmhouse, but more importantly it also takes in Tŷ Mawr, the (rebuilt) birthplace of Bishop William Morgan.

William Morgan, son of a farming tenant of the Gwydir Estate was born in the mid 1540s. Rumoured to have been first taught by a dispossessed monk from Ysbyty Ifan, young William was selected by the powerful Wynn family of Gwydir to be educated by their private tutors. So impressed were they that they sent him to St John's College, Cambridge to study for Holy Orders.

Later when to curb the perceived popish leanings of the Welsh, Queen Elizabeth I, commissioned a translation of the Bible into their own language. The resultant work is attributed to William Morgan and its publication in 1588 codified the Welsh language, combing the classical Welsh of medieval poetry with the language of the hearth and laying down the foundations of modern Welsh literature. The Welsh Bible ensured that Welsh became the language of the new reformed church in

Wales, giving a status to it in an era when it was expelled from law and government in its land. The Welsh language survived, even flourished again, and became the most successful of the six main Celtic tongues and the only one of the three Brythonic ones (Welsh, Cornish & Breton) to be an official medium and to have maintained a significant culture. Although geographical vernacular variations in the language remain, the Bible now used in churches is somewhat revised and the late 20th century resurgence in the use of Welsh has had a purely secular context, the cornerstone of modern Welsh is still the William Morgan Bible.

Curiously Penmachno had two adjacent churches, one St Enclydwyn's (giving the ancient name of the village, Llanenclydwyn), fell into ruin in the 16th century. It is reputedly the burial place of Iorwerth ab Owain Gwynedd, the 12th century ruler and father of Llywelyn the Great. Due to his unfortunate cast of countenance he was called *Drwyndwn* (Flat nose), although presumably addressing him as such risked suffering the same disfigurement! The other church St Tudclyd's rebuilt in the 19th century survives. It has inscribed stones that testify to a strong post-Roman Latin culture.

Penmachno although not obviously industrial, was where the Machno was put to serious work at the woollen mill which although now derelict retains its machinery intact. This together with the ten or a dozen slate workings that despite being tiny, some such as Hwylfa comprising a single workshop cum dwelling, were responsible for the population peaking at 2000. Besides having around 30 shops, there was a bank, a doctor and a dentist, these latter all part-time travelling out from Betws-y-coed on

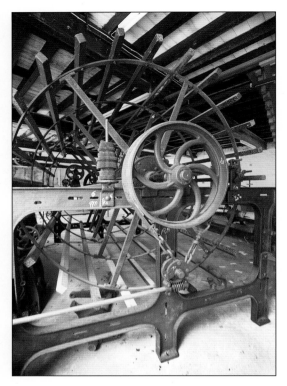

certain days of the week. It had the usual communal bake house and the shoemaker who again really could make shoes. Besides the church there were two chapels, the fine Bethania is no longer used but Salem survives, and its hall/sometime cinema is still the centre of village activities. The Eagles is still open but the Machno Hotel is closed.

Although virtually all traditional trades and occupations have vanished, forestry has gone some way to replacing them. Not just in direct woodland management but in tourism and activities such as mountain biking.

Here the Machno is augmented by Nant y Mynach, ('*monk's stream*') presumably having associations with Ysbyty Ifan, as well as by the Nant Cae Llwyd and more importantly by Afon Glasgwm, that oozes from the peat at Tyddyn Du and makes its way down the Glasgwm valley. Its cataracts incise deep into the rock to reach Penmachno and the Machno near where it passes under the fine three-arch Pont Llan built, as were so many bridges in the late 18th century by local masons. It is quite extraordinary what ambitious structures such as these were built by men who had previously erected nothing larger than a cottage.

Whilst the mason was responsible for the design, the major expense was the construction by the carpenter of the wooden centring on which the initial course of the arch was laid. Thus it was important to remove the centrings intact and at all costs find a buyer who was about to build, or could be persuaded to build, a bridge of similar span or spans.

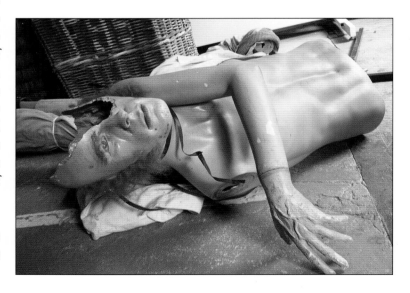

Moving on, the Machno accepts a final top-up from Nant

Caddugan before passing under the sorry remains of a 'Roman' bridge. Little is known of this bridge except that like virtually every other 'Roman' bridge, it is most definitely not Roman. Alongside is the modern replacement, Pont y Pandy, that leads to the old Pandy (fulling) mill and the Conwy Falls and continues on as a back road to Betws-y-coed and on up the southern side of the Lledr valley to join the 'Tŷ Mawr' road. The Cwm Machno road itself crosses the Conwy by the unremarkable Bont Newydd ('*new Bridge*') that shares its unimaginative name with two bridges over Afon Merddwr.

Nearby is the Conwy Falls Café whose 1930s building, an unmistakeable Clough Williams Ellis creation, is the headquarters of 'Go Below' a firm offering underground tours and other adventure experiences.

3
LLEDR

The Lledr rises lonely and isolated on the northern slopes of Moel Fleiddiau to become arguably the most important tributary of the Conwy. Yet it remains an inconsequential collection of streamlets, only becoming a recognisable river when joined by Afon Cwm Edno which drains the granite crag-surrounded Llyn Edno, a lair of trout of allegedly legendary dimensions, although sapient anglers do not dismiss the nearby tiny Llyn Arddu. The Cwm Edno makes a grand sweep past the little Chwarel Owen Parry, where Mr P vainly sought slate and where his trees still attempt to moderate the cutting winds that chilled his long-vanished house. Here the river approximately follows a very ancient route and the nearby poles define the line of the electricity wires from Cwm Dyli power station to a distribution point at Roman Bridge. Part of one of the earliest rural supplies in Wales, these poles were erected on ground so boggy that temporary rail track had to be laid to bring in the materials.

A couple of hundred metres west of where the Cwm Edno begins to swing east at a sheepfold is the memorial to those who died when a Dakota aircraft crashed here in 1952, some of whose 23 victims still lie in the peat. Where the Afon Duweunydd joins, shortly before the river dives into the ravine of Ceunant Ty'n y Ddôl, is the pool that Parry optimistically created to work his hoped-for slate. This pool was later piped for use by the Coed Mawr slate quarry, sited where the Edno joins the Lledr. The Duwaunydd originates at Llynnau Duweunydd that are either two lakes or one hourglass lake according to season. The lake (now in private hands) has brown trout, arctic char and elusive salmon. Like several lakes in Wales, Duweunydd has an *Afanc* legend, referring to a most ugly water-dwelling beast that devoured cattle and humans in equal measure and with equal gusto. Although in this case the legend does not refer directly to these lakes but a particularly nasty example of the species that marauded on the lower Conwy that having been caught and chained was dragged past here by oxen and released in Llyn Glaslyn. Those who doubt this early example of nimbyism are shown the name Bwlch Rhiw'r Ychen ('*pass of the oxen's uphill path*') as proof that this actually took place.

In the meantime the Lledr proper has neared the valley floor and the northern portal of the railway tunnel on the still active Llandudno Junction to Blaenau Ffestiniog line. There are ruins of

an almost monastic-like range of buildings that were the barracks that contractor Gethin Jones built on the ruins of a farm to house his railway tunnellers who toiled for years carving their way to Blaenau through the unyielding rock. Alongside the line are the tips and pits of the Hendre slate working and a little further along the valley road are the remains of the Coed Mawr quarry and the first real settlement, the hamlet of Blaenau Dolwyddelan. Here the Ceunant y Garnedd flows down from Moel Siabod past Garnedd Chapel where that great 19th century orator and campaigning Calvinist, the Reverend John Jones Tal-y-sarn, preached his first sermon. There are vestiges of what is said to be chapel built to cater for needs of the railway navvies, who would not have been welcome at Garnedd.

Joined by Afon Gorddinan, tumbling down to Gorddinan Farm from the heights of Bwlch Gorddinan (the 'Crimea Pass'), the Lledr can rest from its cascading and sedately meander in an orderly fashion to Roman Bridge. The present bridge is obviously far from Roman. The Romans may have built some bridges but not round here – the local Ordoviciae would have knocked them down faster than they could have been erected! Its design betrays its clapper bridge origins following the upper Conwy custom of maintaining the ancient form in modern materials. Roman or not, the railway adopts this name for what must be one of the least used of all railway stations. Although this part of the line passes through slate country, neither quarry in the upper Lledr valley had output that

justified rail connection and the adjacent Penrhiw hone-stone quarry carted through to the Llugwy valley.

It is here that the Lledr having made common cause with the railway is joined by the main road. This road designated a trunk route has had some drastic improvements, but local preservation groups have successfully resisted pressures to comprehensively dual it. Fortunately Pont y Coblyn has now been bypassed thus avoiding the oft repeated 'worst case scenario' of a coach locked in combat with an articulated lorry in its narrow confines.

Together road, railway and river sweep down to Dolwyddelan castle. Revered as the 12th century birthplace of Llywelyn ap Iorwerth (Llywelyn the Great), although he was almost certainly actually born in a wooden structure on the rocky knoll on the valley floor and that he built the present castle as a young man. It effectively controlled two routes into the Snowdon massif, up the Lledr valley and the more difficult but safer route closer to Moel Siabod, as well as providing an 'early warning' lookout for incursions. It remained an important stronghold for Llywelyn's grandson Llywelyn ap Gruffudd (Llywelyn II) until the site was captured by the English by treachery in 1283. Re-garrisoned by Edward I but promptly abandoned when he found that it was only practicable to maintain strongholds that could be supplied by sea, it was re-occupied in the 15th century by Maredudd ap Ieuan, a nobleman from Llŷn with an eye on the main chance. He adapted it into a dwelling but a winter or two cowering within its chill walls convinced him or more probably his wife or wives, (he took a flexible view of matrimony!) that he needed a proper house. He rebuilt a house at Penamnen, whose ruins are still extant. Later as his fortune and his ladies' aspirations grew he took over Gwydir in the lower Conwy valley and founded a great dynasty, his patronymic ap Ieuan being anglicised into Wynn (or Wynne) and adopted as a cognomen.

Visitors to the castle now climb its ramparts and feel a frisson in their feet as they tread the steps scuffed by the shoes of Llywelyn the Great, and feel a shiver of *deja vu* as they peer between the crenulations from where his trusty liegemen discharged their arrows at the Plantagenet incursors. The truth is that much of what you see today is an extensive Victorian restoration by the public-spirited Lord Willoughby de Eresby.

Opposite the castle is the fine monument to John Jones, Tal-y-sarn, in addition a slate plaque on the sidewall of 1 Tanycastell in Dolwyddelan itself is a further memorial. A measure of the influence, status and the respect afforded to John Jones is the vivid picture given of his funeral.

"He died on 16 August, 1857, and was buried at the parish graveyard in Llanllyfni [Arfon]. In the funeral procession were 8 doctors, 65 ministers, 70 deacons, 200 choristers and around 4,000 others with a further 2,000 who joined en route."

By that time the castle was more notable as the location of the Bwlch y Beudy or Chwarel Ddu (*'black quarry'*) so named for the pyretic blackness that characterises the slate produced in the area. It dates from at least the 18th century, but serious exploitation was not possible until 1810 when a road was built from Betws-y-coed enabling their product to be readily carted to Trefriw for loading onto boats on the Conwy. The continuation of this road through the quarry tip and over the Crimea Pass to Blaenau Ffestiniog dates as its name implies from the 1850s. The quarry workings, that were probably the last to use wooden rails, now lie under the castle car park.

Near here the Lledr drove a woollen mill and on the southeast side of the river was another slate quarry, Pompren Fedw. At one time this quarry was owned by Thomas Gee the pioneering publisher and founder of the Gwasg Gee at Denbigh; a somewhat unusual example of diversification.

Dolwyddelan derives its name from the 6th century Irish evangelist St Gwyddelan who settled here and literally means Gwyddelan's Meadow. Curiously although Dôl means meadow archaically it could mean 'loop' and hence might possibly refer to the 'Llan', the circular or ovoid area surrounding a church, which usually prefixes a saint's name to denote a church-nucleated settlement. Presumably for the same reason that pubs are sited at a crossroads to double their passing trade, Gwyddelan staked his claim at an intersection of routes. To the north a street leads on to a track along the line of Afon Ystumiau. To the south the pre-Roman Sarn Helen accompanies Afon Penamnen and was used by slate men trudging over the bare mountain in total darkness, their provisions on their backs possibly in rain or even snow, for their weeklong stint in a dank Blaenau Ffestiniog quarry barracks. Although in more recent times those working in Blaenau itself commuted daily by train, those working in the quarries to the east of Manod Mawr were within living memory still doing the

3.00am Monday morning hike and the Saturday afternoon return.

The present church of St Gwyddelan is not the original, although the hand bell allegedly used by the saint himself to summon the faithful is preserved within it. This current structure replaced one near the castle, being built in the 15th century by Maredudd ap Ieuan allegedly to be handier for his new home at Penamnen. It was extended in the 16th century by Robert Wynne and is a treasure house. The rood screen that was possibly transferred from the previous church is a gem, as are the early 18th century box-pews, pulpit and reading desk. Notable is the roof-beamed carved with the Dolwyddelan Dragon. Such church dragons are said to represent Satan and possibly are a carry-over from heathen times. This one may be connected with the fearsome *Afanc* that may well have personified destructive flooding. The invariably knotted tail seems to heighten its connection with the Welsh Dragon which itself appears in the Roberts window. The 'Clasped Hands' symbol signifying a farewell to earthly life is commonly incised on slate gravestones but in the churchyard here is a most unusual example of the motif inset in marble. A Victorian church intended to replace this one is now a private house.

At Dolwyddelan the detritus of two large slate workings and almost a dozen smaller ones makes the valley unmistakeably industrial. The most obvious, Ty'n y Bryn/Penllyn, was an ancient digging that expanded and prospered mightily when the railway arrived in the late 1870s and was one of only two

workings in Caernarfonshire to have a main line railway siding in its yard. The other large working was Bwlch (Prince Llywelyn) that similarly went for the big time when the railway eliminated cartage to Trefriw, becoming twice the size of Ty'n y Bryn/Penllyn, but unfortunately the days of plenty were few since the great slate boom expired very soon after the railway's opening. Although little remains of Bwlch itself, the tramway embankment that carried block across the valley from Chwarel Fedw for processing in the Bwlch mills is still a delightful feature. Bwlch was powered by tapping into Afon Ystumiau, and Ty'n y Bryn/Penllyn's wheels were turned by yet another Lledr tributary, Afon Bwlch y Groes.

A little further down valley is Pont y Pant where the Sarn Helen goes on its way north-east, which in more modern times was a route walked by slate men from Rhiwddolion in the Llugwy valley to catch the train to Blaenau Ffestiniog after their own quarry Bwlch Gwyn closed during WW1. It is also where Afon Ffridd Carreg y Bwch, a stream not as wide as its name is long, powered the linked slate quarries of Rhiw Goch and Ty'n y Fallen. Developed to take advantage of the railway, they never lived up to either their expectations or their ambitions. A very large mill stands uncompleted and the incline formation that would have carried output down to the railway was never railed. Pont y Pant is a further example of the 'clapper bridge' outline being maintained following rebuild. The nearby footbridge has had its main span replaced but the original slate 'clappers' remain for the approach spans. A little beyond, Afon Wybrnant tumbles in from the south.

Further on is Pont Gethin, the prime edifice of the valley. This viaduct that enables the railway to cross from one side of the valley to the other, must be one of the least photographed structures anywhere in the civilised world, not because of any picaresque shortfall, but because of a plethora of trees and the difficulty of finding a vantage point. Its builder, Owain Gethin Jones sensibly sited

his pillars to suit the terrain resulting in variable spans, the narrowest being the one that goes over the road, so it is under constant threat from the highway planners and it is indeed a traffic bottleneck, but costs dictate that as long as the railway is active this fine structure must remain unsullied. Actually although it looks as solid as anything that Master James of St George put up for Edward I and has been in use for almost a century and a half, the quality of Mr Jones' work did not impress the railway inspectors and some of the 'what the eye does not see' economies in its construction had to be remedied before trains were allowed to use it.

The Lledr having passed under Pont ar Ledr carrying the 'back road' from Penmachno unites with the Conwy at Llyn yr Afanc. The original bridge was erected by Hywel Saermaen (Mason) when the Wars of the Roses were still a tavern topic. His ideas (copied by Jones) of varying the spans of a multi-arched bridges to suit the availability of rock for foundation was continued in its early 18th century replacement.

4
LLUGWY

The Llugwy is the largest of the triumvirate of tributaries that make the Conwy the great river that it is, draining some of the most awesome upland tracts in southern Britain. It enabled Telford to cut his Great Irish Road through the heartlands of Snowdonia, which offered a fine ride on a summer's day but in winter's darkness a different experience. The first twisting miles out of Betws-y-coed climbing westward with horses straining at the collar were perhaps not too bad, certainly for the inside passengers snug behind the lowered window-blinds. But beyond Capel Curig as the flickering warmth of the village and its inn faded behind, the outside passengers must have felt a chill both of temperature and fear as soaked by rain and buffeted by wind, they faced the unknown terrors of Nant y Gwryd. In fact, with the horses being urged to a brisk pace by a brandy-fortified coachman on a dark night on a narrow, rutted road by the light of two candles; fears were not entirely groundless.

The Llugwy originates at Ffynnon Llugwy in a rocky cwm on the bleak slopes of Carnedd

Llywelyn. The name ffynnon suggests a spring but this is a fully-fledged 40-acre lake, the explanation being that until it was dammed in 1919 it was a small moraine-trapped pool that some geologists assert is a vestige of a volcanic crater. Now it is an important water supply that reaches as far as eastern Anglesey, hence the Water Authority's convenient but dauntingly steep access road.

Besides the native brown trout, Ffynnon Llugwy is home to the arctic char, which were re-located from Llyn Peris to escape the disturbance of the Dinorwig pumped-storage scheme. Although elevated it is not quite the highest lake in Wales but here was certainly the highest dwelling, Glyn Llugwy, where at almost 1800' people spent the summer in this Hafod tending their sheep in total isolation.

A weir used to direct the outflow via a grand contour-chasing leat around to Llyn Cowlyd augmenting its contribution to the Dolgarrog hydroelectric generators but nowadays the needs of the householders of Bangor and Menai Bridge take precedence.

On reaching the valley floor, the Llugwy seems to pause as if weighing the attractions of Llyn Ogwen before veering east to accompany the highway. From the south it is augmented by Nant y Gors and Afon Bwlch-goleuni and unnamed trickles that become torrents in the autumnal rains. From the north Afon y Bedol, Ffrwd Goch, Nant Tal y Waun and Afon Llewesig add their quota. The Llugwy passes far below Llyn y Coryn, which is named a lake by the National Park although

its area is a mere tenth of the 2 hectares minimum for official lake status. It lies seemingly fishless glowered over by the crags of Graig y Gigfran ('*raven's rock*') and Graig y Eryr ('*eagle's rock*').

Capel Curig marks the Llugwy's confluence with Nant Gwryd, which although the term Nant (*stream*) might be appropriate as it first cascades from its distant Llyn Cwmffynnon source, it clings to this classification long after it has become a respectable river. Llyn Cwmffynnon was yet another substantial lake that for long was called a spring, being known as Ffynnon Mymbyr when it was included in Llywelyn ap Iorwerth's grant of land to Aberconwy Abbey in the 12th century. Being handy for both the Pen y Pass Youth Hostel and that great climbers' hostelry, the Penygwryd Hotel, the lake's gullible trout are actively and successfully enticed but allegedly due to their inability to distinguish a fly from a 'fly' they never reach maturity, so catches are of unboastworthy dimensions. For those guests looking for more relaxed angling, a Mr Lockwood, a previous keeper of the Penygwryd Hotel, created a lake, which he named with charming lack of modesty after himself. For those of sufficiently non-sedentary disposition, a miner's track (Not to be confused with the Snowdon Miner's Track), can be followed from here up to Bwlch Tryfan a daunting 1500' above and on down into the Ogwen valley.

Nant Gwryd accompanies the road eastwards augmented by Nant Du from the north, Nant y Llys from the south and countless unnamed seasonal torrents. Passing Dyffryn Mymbyr, the homestead famed by James Firbank in *I Bought a Mountain* and through the curious linked lakes, Llynnau

Mymbyr, it reaches the outdoor pursuits centre Plas-y-Brenin at Capel Curig.

Built by Richard Pennant, 1st Baron Penrhyn in 1801 allegedly as a sort of bed & breakfast for guests insufficiently eminent to be accommodated in Penrhyn Castle but actually his purpose was more commercial. As part of the development of his vast estates, including the eponymous slate quarry, the recently ennobled Penrhyn had built a road from Bangor through the Nant Ffrancon pass and Dyffryn Ogwen to Capel Curig to facilitate travel to Betws-y-coed and beyond. The road was rebuilt and partly re-routed by Thomas Telford in the early 19th century and Lord Penrhyn's Capel Curig Inn became a rather posh coaching inn for the Irish Mail. The site was supposedly chosen for its fine views, although coach passengers would be more in need of a lavatory, a fire, a meal and maybe a bed, than a grand vista. When the mail coach was displaced by the railway in 1850, it reinvented itself as the upmarket Capel Curig Hotel for the better class of tourist, including many botanists studying the neo-Alpine flora of Snowdonia. Since guests included Princess (later Queen) Victoria and successive Princes of Wales the name was changed to the Royal Hotel. Of the many famous persons who have stayed here was paradoxically Bishop Samuel Wilberforce, son of William Wilberforce whose success in getting slavery outlawed throughout the British Empire in 1807 is said to have contributed to the apoplectic death of arch anti-abolitionist Lord Penrhyn in 1808.

Although advertised as a 'Resting place for every class of traveller', George Borrow found that when he dined in the 'Grand Saloon' in 1854, his fashionable fellow guests did not subscribe to that motto – *Conceiving that I was some poor fellow travelling on foot from motives*

of economy, they surveyed me with looks of the most supercilious distain. (He might have been wiser to have used the more relaxed Tan y Bwlch Inn.)

In 1955 it became the Snowdonia National Recreation Centre and re-named Plas-y-Brenin (in memory of King George VI). Many outdoor sports are taught and practiced the most high profile being kayaking down waterfalls!

Had any one of several proposals come to fruition, a railway would have accompanied the river along Dyffryn Mymbyr. These schemes involved laying rails up Nant Gwynant from Beddgelert and by a combination of steep grades and a tunnel would have gained Dyffryn Mymbyr and run on through Capel Curig to Betws-y-coed.

Nearer the actual village of Capel Curig, just before the Nant Gwryd joins the Llugwy, the latter is crossed by the Stable Bridge (the name refers to the nearby horse accommodation rather than a guarantee of its rigidity). Close at hand is a 14th or 15th century church *Eglwys Santes Julitta*, probably the smallest in Snowdonia, now deconsecrated and in the care of a local charitable trust it retains, despite alterations and extensions, the traditional 'Double square' layout. In pre-Norman times the dedication of this church, then probably a wattle & daub structure, was to Saint Curig,

Curig the Blessed (*Curig Lwyd*) a 6th century bishop of Llanbadarn. The Normans who of course brought the Celtic Churches within the ambit of Rome, distrusted the genuineness of saints who were not on the Vatican's official list and insisted that the name Curig was a corruption of Cyricus a 4th century infant martyr, so they rededicated the church to him and his mother Julitta. It seems that the recently widowed Julitta had been a Christian activist who fled with the child from Iconium to Seleucia in AD 304 to escape persecution, but found that Alexander the Governor of Seleucia was violently anti-Christian, so she carried on to Tarsus. Like the merchant's servant who on seeing Death in the Baghdad marketplace fled to Samara unknowing that Death had an appointment with him there that night, she found that Alexander was waiting for her at Tarsus. The infant might have been spared had he not attempted to defend his mother from Alexander's enforcers. He was smashed like a doll; his mother was flayed, plunged in boiling pitch, and at last beheaded. Their dismembered bodies were cast into a midden, from where their servants rescued their remains to give them a Christian burial.

At the foot of the mountain, at some distance from the church, stood Gelli'r Mynach, a Middle Ages monk's cell probably attached to the priory at Beddgelert.

A combination of industrial prosperity and increased settlement meant that in 1848 the church, hitherto a daughter church of distant Llandegai, was made a parish church in its own right and eventually a newer and larger church was built, reviving the old St Curig dedication. Also deconsecrated, this newer church has been lovingly converted into a home carefully preserving the fine windows and magnificent *Salvator Mundi* a Venetian mosaic apse. It is now a fine if unusual Guest House.

Apart from the quarries themselves, there is now scant evidence that Capel Curig was an industrial village, even the Ty'n y Coed Inn that once offered liquid sustenance and rough camaraderie to slate quarrymen and lead miners, is metamorphosised into the highly respectable Ty'n-y-Coed Hotel as is Cobden's (neé Tan y Bwlch Inn). A small quarry lies to the west of the village accessed by the tiny but grandly named Pont y Bala (*Bala Bridge*), but the main slate-working activity was on the eastern slopes of Moel Siabod, where the first important digging was Foel. Developed high on the mountainside c1835, it gathered streamlets for power and sent its product down to the road at Pont Cyfyng by a fine rake of gravity-powered inclines. At a lower level was the much larger and later Rhos quarry. Although its output was derisory compared with say Penrhyn, 1000 tons per annum made it a significant producer and although like Cwmmachno it was never rail connected and had to cart its output to Betws-y-coed, it survived. Indeed thanks to the energies of the great

entrepreneur J. J. Riley, it rode out the difficulties of the early 20th century, only finally closing in the 1950s due to a shortage of skilled men rather than lack of business. Its several water wheels included a large example that may have been brought from Cyffty lead mine to power an air compressor, the arrangements to feed these wheels being unusual. Part of Foel was flooded as a reservoir and a dam still impounds water close above the quarry workings; below this is a second (breached) dam built not with stone or earth but with an interesting combination of timber and old rails. A little distance to the southeast is a further reservoir that gathers mountain water. Like other isolated quarries it has buildings that served as barracks or homes according to demand.

Below at Pont Cyfyng on the original road that Telford's construction by-passed, is the quarries' cart loading point and below again alongside the river downstream from the spectacular rapids that serve for hazardous sport and water-rescue training, are the remains of an extra slate processing mill, built by Foel due to a shortage of water at their high mountainside mills. Also at the roadside here is the storage shed for the hones produced at Penrhiw near Dolwyddelan. Nearby is the former Church of St John the Baptist built by a Mr Parry, manager of Rhos quarry to cater for his workforce, is now a private house.

The Llugwy becomes a cascade at Cyfyng Falls and follows the old road past the Roman camp of Bryn-y-Gefeiliau (Caer Llugwy). Originally a 1st century marching camp, it grew into quite an elaborate settlement associated with the lead mining. It has been much degraded and robbed not only of its stone but also of soil, nitrate-enriched by the garrison's al-fresco toilet habits. A hypocaust was covered with slabs of Silurian slate brought from eastern Denbighshire. The local slate was then probably unknown, but the abundant slate of the Ogwen valley, almost within sight of their fort at Segontium (Caernarfon) should have been a handier source. Presumably the natives there were sufficiently unfriendly there to make it inadvisable to venture outside the fort's walls to collect it; making the more peaceful areas of what we now know as Denbighshire a safer source.

Near where the old road is united with the newer one, the river passes under Pont Tŷ Hyll, named after the adjacent 'Ugly House'. This remarkable dwelling, possibly dates from the 15th century, but is unlikely to be, as is often asserted, a 'Tŷ Unnos' – or house built overnight, under an ancient custom that supposedly allowed anyone who built a house with walls, roof and smoking chimney between

sunset and sunrise, to claim the freehold. It is more likely to have been a whimsical fancy and that its original name was Tŷ Llugwy. It is possible that early visitors mistook 'Llugwy house' for 'ugly house'. It is said to have provided shelter for the navvies building Telford's road in the early 1800s. Lived in until c1960, it is now the headquarters of the Snowdonia Society.

Beyond, the river continues until nearing Betws-y-coed, where it abandons all pretence of dignity and torrents in the hugely hyped tripper's destination – Rhaeadr Ewynnol (meaning 'the foaming falls' in Welsh but again mistranslated to 'Swallow Falls' by visitors). Here the river is crossed by the steeply precarious 'Miner's Bridge', that was once the beginning of the miners daily climb to Aberllyn lead mine, high in the forest above.

5
BETWS-Y-COED

Besides being at the confluence with two of its major tributaries, Betws represents a defining point for the Conwy. Upstream, both it and its tributaries are shallow, hurried and abound with white water, downstream it is deep and sedate becoming a trading waterway reaching further inland than any other natural waterway in Wales. Of equal significance is the fact that upstream the river can be readily crossed by bridge, stepping stone or wading. Downstream it generally cannot and thus historically formed a definite and defensible barrier.

This natural barrier is emphasised by the different topography. To the east the heights of the Denbigh moors descend comparatively gently through good agricultural land while to the west daunting scarps rise to hanging valleys and craggy uplands with few agricultural attractions. Thus in ancient times it provided a bulwark against invaders from the east but possibly more importantly,

a discouragement to hungry marauders from the westerly wastes. As Thomas Love Peacock said in an ode that should have cost him penalty points on his poetic licence –

The mountain sheep are sweeter
But the valley sheep are fatter,
We therefore deemed it meeter
To carry off the latter.

Although folk from both banks meet more amicably today one is still aware of a certain frontier town ethos at Betws.

The name Betws-y-coed literally means Prayer House in the Wood, Betws or *Betus* being generally thought to be derived from the Old English *bed-hus* – ie. a bead-house – a house of prayer, or oratory. The surroundings are indeed wooded and it has a Celtic church deriving from a 6th century religious foundation but, prior to the 13th century, the name was Betws Wyrion Iddon, with Wyrion meaning grandchildren possibly suggesting a connection with Iddon, a 6th century King of Gwent, a noted Christian convert.

The church on the river bank near the station, is surrounded by yew trees and is dedicated to St Michael, being until the 16th century a daughter church of the then more important township of Llanrhychwyn. This promotion to parochial status reflects Betws' growth from a mere river confluence to a trading and mining centre. The archangelic dedication of the church represents a transition from the Celtic practice of paying tribute to local saints, to the Norman/Latin practice of using the name of Angels, the Blessed Virgin or of Apostles. Replaced by a Victorian church near the centre of the town, the old now deconsecrated church is another well maintained by a charitable trust.

The 'new' church of St Mary was built on the site of a former cockpit and fairground, and although it is of Early English appearance the internal roof timbers show that it is a modern building. Various types of stone are used in the interior – local bluestone, sandstone and black Cornish serpentine. The square bell tower was added in 1907 and the integral church hall in the 1970s.

Despite being at a natural crossroads, a lack of a market charter restricted Betws' importance and

although miners lived there, the focus of lead mining was at Trefriw. It was only the late 18th century turnpike development and the expansion of coaching that gave the town new importance as well as creating a new type of traveller.

Hitherto, most travel would have been on foot or on horseback and where overnight accommodation was required, it was taken at a rat and flea-ridden inn, probably sharing a room or even a bed with fellow guests. Persons of quality would travel by carriage and since all the 'best' families were interconnected they would normally have relatives with whom they would stay the night. In between these two extremes there were just a few comparatively vermin-free upmarket hotels where mine host would be expected to do some serious grovelling. However such proprietors would be on the lookout for arrivistes in hired turnouts and would examine the coat of arms on the door to ensure it denoted a 'Good' family and not the mock arms of some livery stable, before commencing his obsequies. It was not unknown in the 18th century for persons arriving in a hired equipage at the more pretentious hostelries of snobbish towns to be actually refused accommodation. In fact some guidebooks of the time specified which hotels would accept '*Travellers without their own carriages*'.

The 'Outside' coach passengers might well be persons of humble status, but the 'Inside' passengers

definitely were not, being the 'Platinum Plastic' of the time. These gentry were, thanks to the late 17th century expansion of Dublin and the Irish Act of Union, joined by shed loads of financiers, businessmen, functionaries and opportunists. Some passengers might opt for non-stop travel but those with the means (or expense accounts) would break their journeys to dine at leisure and sleep in a comfortable bed. Such persons would not put up with overnight 'adventures' but demanded a high standard of accommodation, leading to the opening of hotels to what we would now class as 'International standard'. The 1768 Royal Oak at Betws-y-coed whose handsome stables now house the Tourist Office being an example of this new class of hostelry.

Allegedly the 'inventor' of Betws as a resort rather than just an over-nighting place was the distinguished water colourist David Cox, who after several visits took up residence in 1844. Other artists followed so by the time ill-health overtook him in 1856, there was a St Ives-like colony of painters.

Real development of the town began with the arrival of the railway, which gave a new impetus to slate quarrying and lead mining as well as opening up markets for wool and agricultural products. The most overt impact came from the travel possibilities of the 'Penny per mile' 'Parliamentary' trains and more particularly 'Mr Thomas Cook's excursions'. Thus with the growing appreciation that mountains were something to be savoured rather than things that blocked the view, brought Betws a new prosperity. Had it been known what immense

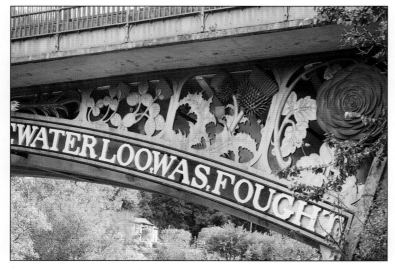

revenues the motor vehicle would bring to the town, a dedication to St Henry (Ford) rather than St Mary might have been more appropriate for the church built to meet the town's expansion.

The centrepiece of the town is Pont-y-Pair (*Bridge of the Cauldron*) that crosses the boiling cataracts of the Llugwy. Yet another of Hywel Saermaen's creations and despite being intended for farm carts, it carried wagons groaning with slate to Trefriw and survives with only minor alterations to carry articulated lorries. Close by this bridge incised into the water-lapped rocks is a 'Rock Canon', a series of 56 holes drilled into the rock that when charged with gunpowder provided (in pre-health and safety times!) a *feu de joie* on joyous public occasions. Here is the start of a pleasant riverside boardwalk.

The pride of the town bridgewise is the Waterloo Bridge built by Thomas Telford as part of his Great Irish Road. Although it crosses the Conwy before it is augmented by the Llugwy, its span exceeds that of the Shropshire Ironbridge upon which is it modelled and is still one of the longest cast iron spans in the country. Unlike bridges of more than 300 years earlier it has had to be substantially re-enforced with concrete. Further downstream is the 'Soldiers' Bridge a modern suspension footbridge that replaced one built by troops during WW1, that in its turn had replaced stepping-stones, vestiges of which are still visible when the water is low.

More visually obvious than the lead mining is Hafodlas slate quarry whose tips push through the trees high above the western extremities of the town. It never achieved the success it deserved or its extensive and innovative infrastructure merited. The quality of its roofing slate was not of the best but towards the end of the 19th century it efficiently turned out the large quantities of cills, lintels, quoins etc that the expanding town demanded. A quite magnificent incline lowered output to road level from where it could be carted to the town and the station. Although at various times owned by railway engineers, including the Great Western's Sir Daniel Gooch it was never directly rail connected. Among early proposals for a line from Conwy to Betws included a branch to the foot of the incline and when all such proposals failed to materialise, it was realised that tonnages would

never warrant the expense of the quarry laying rails themselves.

Like the Rhos workings at Capel Curig, Hafodlas was re-invigorated in the inter-war years by J. J. Riley's happy knack of obtaining support from both capitalists and legislators. Behind the quarry is Llyn Elsi, a reservoir made out of two or three lakelets that is truly 'multi-tasked'. Apart from being a habitat for black-backed gulls it is a fine amenity for walkers and photographers as well as anglers seeking to outwit its brown, rainbow and American brook trout; it also powered the slate quarry and generated electricity to light the town, all in addition to providing a public water supply. The surrounding area is a haunt for mountain bikers and orienteers.

Above Hafodlas is the 'lost village' of Rhiwddolion. Reached by a forestry road that replaced an earlier steep and stony track now unfit for traffic, it is almost devoid of permanent residents. Much is derelict but many of the neat houses have been restored as holiday homes and since most of this hamlet with its chapel (which doubled as a school) nucleated around an excellent example of a Welsh long house, would otherwise be lost, shows the benign side of the 'second home' controversy. A slate-flagged path is a nice feature. The sole *raison d'etre* for this settlement was slate – the Bwlch Gwyn quarry whose pit, tips and tramways are now deep in the trees. When the quarry closed during WW1, many of the men found employment in Blaenau Ffestiniog, walking to Pont y Pant station in the Lledr valley.

Out on the Llanrwst road the less vertiginous visitor can adventure (in safety) among the treetops at Treetops Adventures. Those of a more sedentary disposition can visit the Railway Museum and minature steam railway that occupies the site of the goods yard where slate and wool were once loaded.

6
GARMON

Several millennia before Ffestiniog and Llandecwyn's churchyards provided a 'tomb with a view' and certainly long before the Christian era, Capel Garmon was offering that facility. Its splendidly sited Neolithic burial chamber is as fine an example as can be found anywhere in Britain – in Europe even. It is a communal grave and undoubtedly safeguarded the remains of countless generations who, through cold of winter and heat of summer, had enjoyed the fortunes and suffered the misfortunes of this hilltop place. Although it must be said that not everyone was in awe of its necropollistic associations, since in the 19th century it was used as a stable, presumably on the not unreasonable premise that is was more use to live horses than dead people.

The name Garmon refers to a cell being set up by a St Garmon as a 'branch office' of his foundations at Betws Garmon in Cwm Gwyrfai near Caernarfon, Llanarmon Dyffryn Ceiriog and Llanarmon-yn-Iâl (near Wrexham). This native St Garmon, one of the travelling monks and

preachers who were a part of the Celtic Church should not be mixed up with a more widely known St Germanus, who was a Bishop of Auxerre in Burgundy and who came to Britain in the 5th century to combat the heresies that had arisen in the wake of the Roman withdrawal. He is alleged to have encouraged the local people to resist both the invading Picts who were then pouring across the ungarrisoned Hadrian's Wall, and the Saxons eagerly landing on unguarded shores, each intent on their respective pillagefests. He is said to have organised an ambush, possibly at Maes Garmon near Mold where when the pagan army appeared his followers stoutly cried out 'Alleluia' whereupon the heathen hordes fled.

Capel Garmon did not use the saint's name with the usual 'Llan' prefix since from the saint's time right up to the 20th century it was merely a 'Chapel of Ease' or outstation of Llanrwst. It must be remembered that historically the term 'Chapel (*Capel*) meant a very small church or a section of a larger one, only later being applied patronisingly to non-conformist places of worship. The present church was built at the end of the 18th century close to the site of an early structure that may well have been the actual place where the saint first established himself. In addition to the church, there were three large non-conformist chapels, Seion for the Presbyterians, Bethania for the Wesleyans and Siloam for the Independents. Regrettably the church and two of the chapels are now closed although the fine rectory is still a home.

Capel Garmon is most famous for the Capel Garmon Firedog, a stand decorated with two opposing horned animal heads, found at Carreg Goediog Farm in 1852. It may well have been one of a pair, prominently and proudly displayed on either side of a fireplace as the centrepiece of a home. Modern experiments have shown that to create such an object from ore to finished article, would have taken around three man-years, much more than the house in

which it stood. Such a pair would in modern terms, be in the Bentley bracket. Dating from just prior to the Roman invasion, it demonstrates that even then there were persons able to display conspicuous consumption. The fact that what became the finest Iron Age find in Britian was deliberately buried, suggests some serious reason for doing so. It may have been a votive offering demonstrating extreme allegence to or extreme fear of, some pagan deity. On the other hand it could have been hidden from looters at a time of civil unrest or perhaps anxiety that some Roman official would take a fancy to it. Visitors to the National Museum of Wales can speculate on the possibility of even the most skilled modern craftsman being able to replicate such a piece.

The use of iron as votive offerings stems not just from its cost but also because of the apparent

magical powers of the smiths who made them. The smith's abilty to bend iron to his will by the use of fire, and his fearlessness in the face of flame, led to a suspicion that his powers had infernal origins. In addition, on droving routes the smith would shoe cattle which was done with the beast lying down. Persuading a steer that had no wish to assume a recumbent posture to do so, called for strength of both arm and character, futher emphasising that the smith was a man best not to cross. In any case, the smith was pivotal to village life – you could manage without a vicar but you could not manage without a smith.

Whilst the practice of naming chapels after Biblical locations is not confined to Wales, it is very much a Welsh practice. Often built in remote locations, either to be central for a widely scattered congregation, or where a landowner could be persuaded to risk the wrath of the Establishment and sell a plot on which to build. Settlements would accrete around the chapel usually adopting its biblical name – as in the case of nearby Nebo village.

Nebo is little more than a hamlet, but it is the reputed site of the *Maen Sertan* (boundary stone) or *Maen-y-Siarter* – (charter stone) named in the 1198 charter granted to Aberconwy Abbey. Apparently it was not unusual for an abbey to have sites such as this to act as out stations where baptisms could be performed and blessings conferred.

Admittedly the waterfalls on this side of the valley are smaller than those to the west, but they do have their attractions – such as where Gallt y Gwg tumbles or Afon Cyffdy cascades its Denbigh Moor drainings through Nant-y-rhiw or where Afon Sychnant passes through Nant Bwlch y

Gwynt to become Nant y Goran to drive the Melin-y-coed mill. This 18th century mill is a re-build of a much earlier mill and is really the sole reason for the village's existence, consisting as it did of Mill Bank House, a handfull of cottages, Bethel Presbyterian Chapel, a farm or two and the mill itself; all presided over by the 16th century Cyffdy Hall with its magnificent Douglas Fir avenue. The miller was another key community figure, who far from sitting watching corn go in at the top and flour come out at the bottom, had the skilled and onerous tasks of re-cutting worn millstones and carving replacements for worn gear-wheel teeth from a nearby apple, cherry or hornbeam tree.

The Denbigh moors to the east may be less intimidating than the wild heights to the west of the river but save where they are despoiled by wind turbines, are a tract of singular beauty. Unsurprisingly they are a place where fact and fantasy intermingle.

Unlike say the Migneint, they do not have a history of thieves and vagabonds, allegedly because it is patrolled by the shade a Roman Centurion.

For I am a man under authority, having soldiers under me: and I say to this man, Go, and he goeth; and to another, come, and he cometh; and to my servant, Do this, and he doeth it. (The Centurion: Matthew 8.9)

It has been suggested that he was the sole surviver of a detachment ambushed and slaughtered, and having lost all of the eighty men for whom he was responsible, was condemned to wander here to expiate his disgrace without even the sustenance of a sandwich garnished with *Garum* (the fish sauce, relished by Romans but by no one else).

When the wind is from the right direction the clank and creak of his accoutrements can be clearly heard and in the eeriness of night his presence can be felt but few have actually seen him. This is indeed fortunate since to even glimpse the helmet with the officer's crest and the silvered armour, presages certain death. Although confirmation of any of this is hard to find, there are those who are reluctant to travel on the lesser-used moorland roads after nightfall.

7
GWYDIR

The Conwy, having assembled its main tributaries at Betws-y-coed, changes character completely. Gone are the ravines and white water; from here the river flows with measured dignity.

To the west is a scarp; above which afforested high ground leads to the 'Lake District' of Wales, where more than a score of lead mines have left buddles, crusher houses, tramways and heaps of tailings lurking in the woodlands. There was slate too and in fact some of the earliest slate workings in Wales were in this lower Conwy valley and it once stood on equal terms with northwest Gwynedd as a slate area. Unfortunately from the late 18th century it was increasingly overshadowed by better, more abundant and more readily transported slate from other parts of Wales.

As soon as the railway was laid through Conwy town in 1848 on its way to Holyhead, there were immediate plans to run a branch line up the valley but it would be a dozen years before the present-day line opened. Being laid to the east of the river enabled Trefriw to retain some slate, lead

and pyrites traffic, but it lost its main trade, the slate, lead and wool and other produce from the Llugwy, Lledr and Machno valleys which would now be loaded onto rail at Betws-y-coed.

The proprietarily focus of the area was Gwydir Castle, the centre of an estate stretching far up the Lledr and Llugwy valleys. Lying as Leland said '*Two bowshots above the river Conwy*', the castle was the home of the influential Earls of Ancaster, a branch of the all-pervading Wynn family. The first castle was built by Hywel Coetmor who commanded bowmen under the Black Prince at Crecy during the Hundred Years War, and was a captain in Owain Glyndŵr's war of independence. Following the Wars of the Roses it was rebuilt as a fortified manor house by Meredudd ap Ieuan the founder of the Wynn dynasty as a grand replacement for his Dolwyddelan premises. In the more settled times of the 16th century, using materials 'salvaged' from the destruction of Maenan Abbey, it was extended as a normal mansion, if indeed normal can be applied to such a magnificent pile.

Gwydir became a centre of scholarship, encouraging suitable local lads to pursue higher education (such as Bishop Morgan). It was the one-time home of Katherine of Berain, a cousin of Elizabeth I and was connected with the Queen's adviser, the Earl of Leicester. Charles I stayed here,

as did King George V and Queen Mary. Although there have been alterations and additions, including 19th century work by Sir Charles Barry the architect of the Houses of Parliament, this remains one of the finest examples of a Welsh Tudor courtyard house. The (still ongoing) renovation by painter and architectural historian Peter Welford and his writer and book restorer wife Jenny Corbett, is one of the most ambitious ever undertaken by private individuals. The 17th century Dining Room panelling that had been pillaged in the 1920s by William Randolph Hearst was bought from the Metropolitan Museum of New York, enabling the room to be refurbished and opened by the Prince of Wales. The house and grounds are open to the public and offer various types of holiday accommodation.

The great gem of Gwydir is the 17th century Gwydir Uchaf Chapel (not to be confused with the Gwydir chapel of Llanrwst Church). This one has a quite magnificent, painted barrel-roof depicting the Creation, the Trinity and the Last Judgement – a sort of miniature Sistine Chapel. Behind the Castle are the fine woodlands (Coed Garreg y Gwalch) accessible by steep lanes, which give onto the desolate uplands beyond.

The original parochial centre was Llanrhychwyn, its church said to be the oldest in Wales, was founded in the 6th century by St Rhychwyn of the royal house of Llys Helig which was on land now drowned near Penmaenmawr.

The Topographical Dictionary of

Wales of 1849 described the hamlet –

"*This parish of 551 inhabitants, which is exceedingly mountainous, contains an abundance of pyrites, worked by a company from Liverpool, who ship the produce at the adjoining quay of Trefriw. There are also three extensive slate-quarries within its limits, at the distance of about one mile and a half from the shipping-place, in which upwards of 100 persons are employed; (Clogwyn y Fuwch, Pen y Ffridd and possibly Tal-y-bont?) lead-ore has been obtained here, and some small veins of it are now being worked. Numerous varieties of quartz crystals are found, some of them of a beautiful amethystine colour, and of considerable value. The church is situated among barren mountains, at a considerable distance from any houses, and, from the rudeness of its architecture, appears to be of great antiquity. It is vulgarly observed of this simple structure, that it was erected prior to the invention of the saw and plane, since no indication of the use of these instruments can be discovered in any part of the edifice. In the east window are the remains of some handsome stained glass, with a mutilated date, which seems to have been MCCCCXXII (1422).*

There are one or two places of worship for dissenters, by whom five Sunday schools are supported; and two trifling bequests producing about 13s per annum, are distributed among the poor at Christmas.

70

This somewhat unfortunately worded summary fails to mention the unusual stone font, the wooden door-hinges or the fine roof beams of the mainly 12th century church or its 17th century fittings. The bell is believed to have been taken from Maenan Abbey when it was 'going spare' after its Dissolution.

In the sweep of woodland behind Gwydir, lakes predominate; nearest to Gwydir is the elongated Llyn Parc a natural lake dammed as a reservoir to drive the wheels and turbines of the Aberllyn lead and zinc mine. Its lead content precludes fish but it is said that the red squirrel can be seen. To the west of the lake is a wall built by Napoleonic prisoners of war to contain the deer in the then Gwydir Park."

There are a number of small mine-related impoundments which are the haunts of waterfowl, the largest being Llyn Ty'n y Mynydd that supplied the Cyffty lead mine, whose unique remains were regrettably bulldozed and landscaped in 1966. Nearby is the larger Llyn Sarnau, also a mine reservoir. Llyn Bychan the similarly sized but natural lake is far enough from mineralisation to support brown trout. Llyn Pencraig is larger (in the winter at least) and supposedly has otters, but its fish are mainly tiddlers too small to interest serious anglers. Traditionally this lake was once a good deal bigger and called Llyn Llifon after the stream Gwaen Llifon. Llyn Goddionduon is more substantial and a real brown trout lake, one of several lakes owned by Cobden's Hotel at Capel Curig for the use of their guests. Llyn Bodgynydd whose waters helped to turn the water wheels at Pandora lead mine is much smaller but is still a good sporting lake. Llyn Glangors is largely artificial which, like its attendant lakelets was part of the supply system for Pandora and Hafna lead mines. For a short time in the 1980s it was a nursery for a smoked salmon business, but is now private fishing.

There are other lead/zinc mines such as Llanrwst and Klondyke with substantial surface remains; all save Parc closed in the 1920s, this latter clinging to survival into the 1960s. The whole area is now excellent mountain bike territory.

The 'Great Lakes' of the area are Llyn Geirionydd and Llyn Crafnant. The road on the southern shore of Geirionydd

follows the route of the tramway that carried lead ores from the Willoughby mine to the head of a ropeway down to the Klondyke mine where several buildings survive, but not of course the gold dust with which the mine was once 'salted' to encourage potential investors. On the western shore of the lake was a small Wolfram (Tungsten) mine but it also has a more cultural connection. A monument on Bryn y Caniadau ('hill of songs') the hillock near the lake's outfall commemorates the 6th century poet Taliesin who allegedly composed verses in the tranquillity of the lakeside. Eisteddfodau were held here in the late Victorian era and there are associations with both the bard and hymnist Ieuan Glan Geirionydd and the blind harpist David Francis from Blaenau Ffestiniog. The lead content causes fish to be sparse, but there are plenty of other activities that regrettably now include water-skiing thus destroying the tranquillity savoured by Taliesin and valued by countless others since.

Crafnant, like Geirionydd, is accessible by car and a circuit of its shores makes a fine bird-watching walk. A monument commemorates the lake having been donated to enable it to be damned to provide a free domestic water supply to Llanrwst. Unhappily by some sleight of hand the good folk

of Llanrwst now have to pay their Water Rates like the rest of us. The absence of lead workings in Crafnant's immediate proximity enable it to have an abundance of trout, but there were several slate quarries in its valley. Manod and Cornel were relatively unremarkable, but bigger and with cavernous underground workings Clogwyn y Fuwch is a prominent landscape feature. Clogwyn was laid out and operated in the Lakeland manner, giving rise to an unsubstantiated belief that men from northwest England opened it. Near Llanrhychwyn are the eerie and enigmatic caverns of Pen y Ffridd quarry, an early 18th century working, it was the largest slate undertaking on the lower Conwy in its 19th century heyday and may have been the first underground working in Wales. The near dozen other slate workings were small and most suffered early extinction due to a combination of poor quality and even poorer transport. Tal y Llyn quarry south east of Geirionydd was a little more substantial than most as was Cae Rhobin near the Cae Coch pyrites mine.

Sir John Wynn referred to this pyrites mine in 1607, writing —

"A great store of brimstone (Sulphur). It may be digged at a small charge and lies within two bowshots of a navigable river which, within seven miles, empties itself into the sea."

This mine was redeveloped in 1817 by Thompson & Hill, a London firm who were relocating their sulphur manufacture to Liverpool. Under various owners up to more than 100 men were employed until the 1890s. Resurrected in 1917 to meet wartime needs, power plant, compressors, a crushing mill and an aerial ropeway to carry the pyrites across the Conwy valley to the railway line were constructed and a workforce of 230 taken on but it was closed 2 years later. Underground the microorganisms living in the highly acidic slimes are brilliantly coloured in reds and yellows and are of great biological interest but can rot the boots off one's feet!

8
LLANRWST & TREFRIW

Llanrwst people speak of *Cymru, Lloegr a Llanrwst* (Wales England and Llanrwst) tacitly according statehood to the town – a sort of riverside Monaco. Although applications to be separately represented at the United Nations have so far failed, the claim may have historical precedent. Allegedly when Gwynedd was divided up between the fifteen Noble Tribes, the parish of Llanrwst was accidentally omitted, alternatively it may derive from 1276 when Llywelyn ap Gruffudd (son of Llywelyn the Great) believing that bandits and wrongdoers were being allowed to abuse the parish's right of sanctuary declared it independent of the see of St Asaph.

Situated on the eastern bank of the Conwy river, it stands on a ford 11 miles from Conwy town and castle, the colonial centre of Edward I and his occupying forces. Edward commanded that no Welshmen could buy or occupy property or business in his priviledged towns, and that the Welsh farmers of the area could not set up a rival market of their own within 10 miles of their boundaries.

Since Llanrwst was just outside Edward's 'exclusion zone' a rival market was established there which enabled Llanrwst to become a much more significant market town than Conwy. Although occupied by foreign armies from time to time, and burnt to the ground by Henry IV in 1402, it remained a rebel town, outside the stronghold of the mountains to the west, but fiercely independent. The saying *Cymru, Lloegr and Llanrwst* came to honour its history and celebrate its character. Llanrwst was at one time the eighth largest town in Wales much outshining the village of Cardiff and is still undisputedly the 'Capital' of the lower Conwy valley.

Wool and the knitting of stockings played a big part in the town's economy and the 'Llanrwst Price' effectively set the levels obtained for woollen goods throughout Britain. Even more renowned was the making of harps, the small, portable harps that are so embedded in the Welsh psyche, and are the basis of the Welsh musical tradition with a subliminal Biblical association with Lake Geneseret (Lake of the Harp – Lake Galilee).

The Llanrwst area was also known for its clocks, the first being made by Watcyn Owen in the earliest years of the 18th century although it was his great, great grandson also Watcyn who at the end of that century became the prolific clockmaker. Unlike some clock makers he believed that the quality of the case should match that of the movement. Using his connections with the Gwydir estate he ensured that of the oak sent downriver to Liverpool for sawing, only the finest planks would eventually return for the making of clock cases and clock-incorporating furniture. He built up a network of

outworkers making components enabling several dynasties of clockmakers to emerge both from his family and from ex-employees. The antique shop often has a Llanrwst clock in stock and the town clock with its eagle weather vane also reminds us of the town's horological pedigree.

Nant y Glyn (Afon Bach) tumbles into the town, having done it's milling on the way, but no longer has a brewery or a tannery to supply; fortunately the tannery that closed in 1979 has been preserved and restored. With so much thirst inducing tanning, lead mining and slate quarrying in the district the number of public houses almost outstripped the private houses.

Llanrwst's traditional printing happily continues, and with it the combining of printing with poetry pioneered across the river at Trefriw in the 18th century by Dafydd Jones (*Dewi Fardd*). Since both printing and versifying are less physically demanding than the old heavy occupations, most of the inns and alehouses are now closed. The old Union Inn, once the 16th century Post House, has become Pickwick's café and shop. In its yard, once the scene of early Methodist meetings, is a well that probably pre-dates every building in the town.

Success was not without setbacks. In the 10th century, the town was fought over in the Battle of

Llanrwst when the princes of the north successfully trounced the troops of the sons of Hywel Dda who had moved in from the south. In the 13th century there were harvest failures throughout the Conwy valley; families fled and the town languished but eventually recovered only to be all but destroyed in the mid 14th century by the Black Death. Walled and controlled towns such as Conwy escaped the worst, but at Llanrwst contaminated by the very travellers and traders that created its prosperity, it is said that the unburied dead outnumbered the poor wretched survivors.

It took 50 years for the town to even start to recover from this scourge only to find itself in the midst of the Glyndŵr uprising. Since Hywel Coetmor of Gwydir were Glyndŵr's most loyal supporters, Henry IV dealt savagely with the town, putting it to the torch and slaughtering its inhabitants. Just a few citizens were able to escape to live like outlaws in the woods. Scarcely recovered from this, the good folk of Llanrwst were then involved in the Wars of the Roses on the Lancastrian side which did not best please the Yorkist Earl of Pembroke who again laid waste the town, this time burning down the thatched-roof 12th century church of St Grwst.

These vicissitudes are now commemorated by the Gateway sculptures that greet the traveller at either end of the town. Both are a tight cluster of tall, bleached tree trunks that appear to be frozen

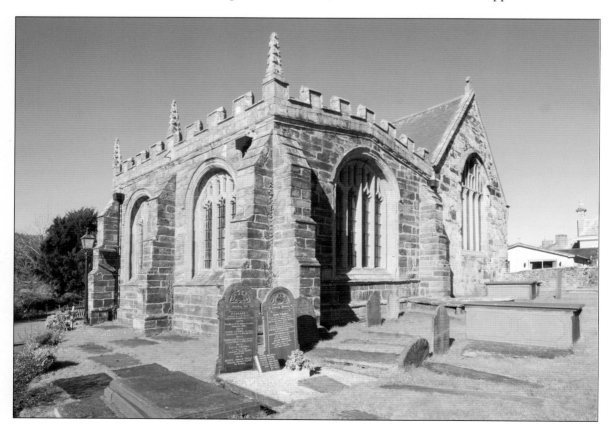

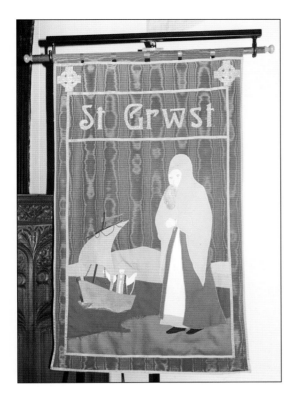

in a uniformly curving, permanently wind-bent position. They were carved by Cardiff-based Nigel Talbot from Welsh oak trees selected for the precise angles of their branches. Each trunk also has a small cast-metal, low relief panel set into its surface, representing the history of Llanrwst. These were designed and made by young people from local schools and youth clubs.

The present church, which is a 17th century rebuild of the one that replaced the victim of the pyromanically inclined Pembroke, has a rood screen probably moved here from Maenan Abbey. The fine carved-ceilinged Gwydir chapel adjacent is an addition by Sir Richard Wynn as a mausoleum for himself, sadly he lived to see all his five sons buried and memorialised there. There is also an effigy of Hywel Coetmor but more importantly it contains the stone coffin of Llywelyn the Great that came from Maenan Abbey having been previously in the original Aberconwy Abbey. St Grwst has the advantage over some Welsh saints in that he is a documented historical figure. With Royal connection and related to many Celtic leaders, Grwst enjoyed much standing and eminent people travelled long distances to consult him on spiritual matters, earning him the title of Grwst the Confessor. The site of his cell and 6th century church are thought to have been near Seion chapel and the housing estate Cae Llan ('church field'). A second church, St Mary's now demolished, was opened in 1842 mainly to cater for English speakers.

On the approach to St Grwst's church are the Almshouses built in 1610s by Sir

John Wynn the first Baronet of the upwardly mobile Gwydir family to house the poor and needy. Originally collectively known as *Ysbyty Iesu* (Jesus Hospital), they closed when the last inmate Mary Roberts died in 1976. The almshouses were associated with the neighbouring Grammar School, the Headmaster doubling as their Warden. The fine structure has been restored and houses a small museum that commemorates the social, artistic and industrial life of the town. As elsewhere, the once-proud non-conformist denominations are in retreat, some chapels such as Capel Coch have found other uses, but of Tabernacl only the graves remain.

The most famous landmark is the town bridge built of slate and gritstone probably to replace an earlier wooden structure. It was reputedly designed by Inigo Jones, as a visitor to Gwydir it is possible that he had some hand in at least its ornamentation. Almost as soon as it was built, the western end was blown up by Royalist forces trying to prevent the Roundhead artillery from reaching Conwy castle. Officially known as *Pont Fawr* although *fawr* (big) it is definitely not. Humped-back and so narrow that motorcyclists tuck in their elbows and, despite traffic lights, it can be the scene of acrimonious headlamp-to-headlamp vehicular confrontations, and the confidence of pedestrians cowering in the refuges is not helped by the allegation that a stout thump on the parapet will cause

the whole structure to vibrate. That said, it is a most elegant and oft-depicted construction that bears loads undreamt by whoever did design it, and has suffered countless disastrous floods that would have carried away a lesser edifice. Built in 1636, a time when the Wynns of Gwydir were politically on thin ice, Sir John Wynn having been a notable absentee at the 1605 opening of Parliament, allegedly because a relative, the secretly papist curate of Trefriw, had warned him of the Gunpowder Plot. Wisely Sir John as the bridge's sponsor took the opportunity to demonstrate his loyalty to the Stuart cause by having the arms of both Charles I and his Prince of Wales son inscribed upon it. The sundial seems an anachronistic survivor but was put there in 1936 to celebrate the bridge's tri-centennial.

At the far end of the town bridge is *Tu Hwnt i'r Bont* a 15th century farmhouse now run as a tearoom by the National Trust. For long it acted as a courthouse although the Law it administered was liable, one suspects, to be that of the Wynns rather than that of the Land, as inferred by Thomas Pennant –

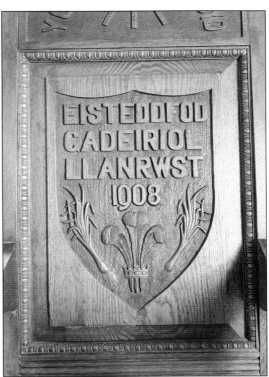

"*When steel-shod cattle crossed the ford, and the valley ruled by a well-wined Lord;*

I stood a Court House, cold and grave, as dismal as old Siencyn's Cave;

On yonder crag I spelt the Law, an object of pity, spile and awe;

And many a knarled and trembling hand, In terror gripped the witness stand;

As empty-gloried tyrants sat, and on their fellow mortals spat;

Their bride-horned justice, dark the day. Where the

Wynn's of Gwydir held their sway."

The railway that secured Llanrwst's fortunes was originally planned to closely follow the riverbank in anticipation of which a large hotel designed and fitted out to the highest standards was built opposite what was to be the station concourse. Sadly the Victoria Hotel finally gave up awaiting a flood of First Class passengers and was demolished in the 1990s. Although the railway did run conveniently close to the town, perversely the station was located some distance off, and it was only in 1989, in response to the requirements of the Eisteddfod the present Denbigh Street station was opened. The original station was retained as a request halt renamed as Llanrwst North, so providing the town with the dignity of two stations, giving a vision of a passenger buying a through ticket from say, Omsk being asked "Would that be Llanrwst or Llanrwst North?"

The second river crossing is a footbridge replacing the wooden road bridge erected by the redoubtable Reverend John Gower, Rector of Trefriw, to enable the formations of an abortive Llanrwst to Trefriw rail line proposal to be used as a carriageway enabling visitors arriving at Llanrwst station to be driven to Trefriw (and some say to encourage Llanrwst churchgoers to attend his services).

This route was apparently a boon to persons transiting between the two towns during the hours of darkness since it obviated the danger of wandering into the territory of the Tylwyth Teg (fairies). Since Dyffryn Conwy fairies were it seems, less mischievous than some in other places, more notorious misdemeanours such as the substitution of piglets for babies were rare, but they fiercely guarded their own privacy. Should a young man of good countenance stumble into one of their rings, he would be liable to find himself seized by fairy girls who would hold him captive and have their wicked way with him for a year and a day.

Trefriw, the highest point on the Conwy that could be reached by sea-going vessels, was where lead, slate and agricultural products were craned aboard the ships that brought in necessities and manufactures. Trefriw handled the output of the innumerable Gwydir lead mines, but overwhelmingly it was a slate port. Not only was the product of the quarries of the Conwy valley and its tributaries loaded there, but also a great deal from those in the Blaenau Ffestiniog area that could not readily reach the Ffestiniog Railway. Its mid-19th century peak of over 16,000 tons p.a. made it one of the major ports of Wales with up to 450 ships trading there.

Trefriw provided homes and lodgings for the lead miners and slate quarrymen and had a

number of small industries of which the now not-so-small woollen mill is the sole survivor. Like the now defunct factories it is powered by the waters of Afon Crafnant, one of the larger of the many torrents that cascade down the scarp forming waterfalls such as the 'Grey Mare's Tail'.

In earlier times Trefriw had outshone Llanrwst, it being where Llywelyn the Great built a hunting lodge, but his wife Siwan stood on her dignity as a daughter of King John of England and jibbed at the climb to Llanrhychwyn church so he had to build a church specially for her (St Mary's Trefriw, subsequently much rebuilt). Siwan's distaste for barons ("*so beastly to Daddy at Runnymede*"), failed to discourage her from extending the hospitality of her bedchamber to their son Dafydd's prospective father-in-law, William, Baron De Braose, when he came to stay. A week or two after accepting this Celtic courtesy, William was found mysteriously hanged. Presumably royal connections saved Siwan from a similar fate.

The plummeting of Trefriw's fortunes as a port following the opening of the railway caused it to seek an alternative role as a resort and spa town exploiting the abundant iron-rich waters that once fortified weary Romans. Although its pump room and curative baths were less commodious and

never as well patronised as its 19th century contemporaries at say Harrogate or Llandrindod, its waters were said to be to be equally efficacious as a cure for most of mankind's physical frailties. Some of its propaganda was a touch over-the-top as was written in 1879 –

"Regarding the village itself, its position is such that germs cannot live in it – every part of it is on a self-purifying slope – its pure and balmy air, and its beautiful aspect, it receives the healthiest greetings of the morning sun, so that it fully justifies its title – the healthiest place in Wales".

Later, much was made of the longevity of Mary Owen who was born at Trefriw in 1803 and lived to the age of 108. Although she spent almost all her life on Anglesey, Trefriw steadfastly claimed her as one of their own.

Nowadays claims are more modest and do have medical endorsement, thus Trefriw Spa continues to supply its *Spatone* product to devotees worldwide.

When it became apparent that Trefriw would not be rail-served, the Reverend Gower's bridging initiative helped to attract visitors, but the grand way to reach Trefriw was by steamboat from Conwy Quay, landing at Trefriw Quay, which was, but a short step to the Bellevue Hotel (later renamed The Prince's Arms in deference to Llywelyn,). This service was started in 1847 by the paddle steamer *St Winifred* that was eventually joined by four further vessels, mostly carrying day-trippers so that at holiday times in the early years of the 20th century, the town was almost trampled to death by up to 1000 excursionists. Although in the 1950s some attempt was made to run a motorboat service, passenger carrying effectively ceased with WW2. The quay once so commercially active is now completely deserted and its beautiful ceramic walls overgrown.

9
DOLGARROG

Afon Porth Llwyd and Afon Ddu are two of the principal western tributaries of the lower Conwy, draining some of the dramatically bleakest tracts in southern Britain. Both drove flour mills near Porthllwyd at what is now Dolgarrog, one of which diversified into paper making supplying some of the earliest printers such as Dafydd Jones of Trefriw, its building doubling up as one of the first non-conformist Sunday schools in Wales. In addition, in the mid-19th century, a water-powered sawmill exploited the local woodlands to meet the huge demand for railway sleepers.

At the beginning of the 20th century aluminium was being seen as the metal of the future but smelting it called for prodigious quantities of electricity. This meant that only cheap hydro-electricity could keep the metal's cost within bounds. British Aluminium, seeking a suitable smelting site, recognised the potential of the Porth Llwyd and the Ddu, opening a works at Dolgarrog in 1907.

Whilst the two main rivers were the primary sources of water, they were augmented from the

north by tapping into Afon Dulyn and from the south Afon Llugwy and their respective associated streams. A combination of tunnels and open leats enabled every drop of water to be wrung from a 7 or 8 miles fan of catchments feeding three reservoirs. The lowest reservoir Coety, is a largely artificial lake at the head of an impressive gorge, now much used for climbing and adventure training. A few hundred yards to the southeast of the lake are traces of a medieval community. Wiped out by the Black Death and never re-occupied, its replacement settlement being established nearer the valley floor.

Coety basically was intended as a 'header tank' for the Dolgarrog turbines, being fed from Cowlyd, which is an ancient fishing lake enlarged by a massive dam into one of the biggest and deepest in Snowdonia. Its antiquity has attracted legends from many sources including the Mabinogion, the 14th century writings based on oral accounts from much earlier times. In one of the stories Culhwch has to complete a number of tasks to win the hand of Ysbaddaden's daughter Olwen, for which he enlisted the help of King Arthur. For one of these tasks, the finding and liberation of the imprisoned son of Maldron, he is said to have consulted various creatures including the 'Owl of Cwm Cowlyd'.

"Owl of Cwm Cowlwyd, here are Arthur's messengers, Knowest thou aught of Mabon son of Modron, who was taken from his mother when but three nights old?"

"If I knew I would tell it, when I first came hither the great valley was a wooded glen. And a race of men came thereto and laid it waste."

Whatever the truth of the legend it does suggest that this now billiard-ball bare tract was de-forested by early settlers, and indeed the whole has traces of pre-historic occupation.

The rising ground behind the lake is Pen Llithrig y Wrach (the slippery top ground of the witch). Whilst we do not know anything of a witch, there are Celtic tales of giant hags who could escape apprehension by sliding down hillsides and that screes are evidence of their passage. Cowlyd has its 'Water Bull' legend, commonplace in parts of Ireland but unusual in Wales. Clearly a variation on the *Afanc* myths, whereby a creature emerges from the depths and carries away unwary passers-by. It is also *Tylwyth Teg* territory – the evilly mischievous beings whose amusement was to make life difficult for humans, particularly any that failed to show them proper respect. However it must be said that if they took a liking to you, your crops would thrive and your flocks multiply. Specific to

Cowlyd is the tale of a *Tylwyth Teg* woman bathing her infants in the lake using a magic soap even a trace of which would blind a human eye – or least prevent that eye seeing things that did not want to be seen – which is said to account for sightings of fairies being so rare.

The third major lake is Llyn Eigiau, a most curious stretch of water, which replenishes Cowlyd via a tunnel. It is again an enlargement of an ancient lake that was spoken of in the 17th century as having 'shoals' of fish. It indeed has small brown trout and allegedly Arctic char, but it is mainly remembered for its dam failure of 1925. With the lake now drained down almost to its pre-impoundment size, one can see that the dam was little more than a garden wall. Small wonder that following torrential rain, there was a catastrophic failure that allowed water to rush down the valley into Llyn Coety breaching its dam. The augmented torrent overwhelmed much of Dolgarrog village, but fortunately most of the people were at the weekly 'moving picture' show at the hall on higher ground but even so 16 lives were lost. There are tales, many probably apocryphal of the church bell tolling as it was swept away and of people clinging to furniture and singing hymns as they were carried along the Conwy. The swathe of debris-strewn destruction is still to be seen. Also

in the peat hereabouts are tree stumps, showing that a milder climate once enabled trees to flourish at this height.

Above Eigiau are two of the most remote lakes in Snowdonia, Dulyn and Melynllyn. In 1807 it was said of the dark and glowering cliff-encircled Lake Dulyn –

"There is a lake in the mountains of Snowdon, called Dulyn, in a rugged valley, encircled by high steep rocks. This lake is extremely black, and its fish are deformed and unsightly, having large heads and small bodies. No wild swans are ever seen alighting upon it (such as are on all the other lakes in Snowdon), nor ducks, nor any bird whatever. And there is a causeway of stones leading into this lake; and if any one goes along this causeway, even when it is hot sunshine, and throws water so as to wet the furthest stone, which is called the Red Altar [Yr Allor Goch], it is a chance if it do not rain before night."

The fish in this lake, which has been a water supply for Llandudno since the 1880s, are of course perfectly formed brown trout and arctic char. It is said that the appearance of a dove portended the death of a witch and if an ungodly person was to venture to its edge he (no she's apparently) would be dragged in to drown. If one spent a night here on May Day, Midsummer or Halloween, one would be made aware of every impending death. What is more factual is that close to the lake there were 19th century trials for hone stones (for sharpening tools) and sadly in the 20th, up to a score of aircraft were wrecked here, most without survivors. The smaller but even higher Llyn Melynllyn, also the site of several air crashes, has the usual brown trout and arctic char awaiting those hardy anglers prepared to face the

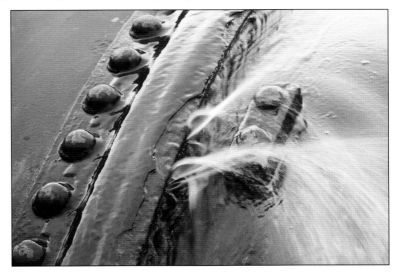

2000' ascent from the Conwy valley. It was also a working lake, supplying via a leat, the Melynllyn hone quarry whose tramway formation from mine to mill is traceable. The wrecked mill that still has remnants of machinery must have been one of highest 'factories' in the country.

These lakes are backdropped by Carnedd Gwenllian, neé Garreg Uchaf, belated renamed to honour the only child of Llywelyn the last legitimate Prince of Wales. When Llywelyn was killed Gwenllian still an infant was seized and incarcerated for life by Edward I to clear the way for him to declare his own son Prince of Wales.

In the Cwm beyond Llyn Eigiau, there were two slate quarries, Cedryn and Cwm Eigiau. Both have extensive remains of mills, inclines and so on that reward industrial archaeologists prepared to make the tiresome trudge. At least they can drive partway, but the quarrymen had to walk at least five hard uphill miles from the valley villages carrying their week's provisions on their backs. Even this task was exceeded by that of the Bethesda men who had to walk even further over the bare mountain, reaching 3000' possibly in winter darkness. Either way they would have to arrive by 7am on a Monday morning to spend five tough days in a verminous barracks.

In the 1860s these two quarries built a narrow gauge tramway to the river near Dolgarrog. It followed the valley floor in a gentle descent, apart from one short incline, to the cusp above Dolgarrog from where it dropped to the Conwy flood plain by a series of three gravity inclines, passing under the road and thence to a landing stage on the river. When the quarries closed some 20 years later, the tramway was far from done for. To assist with the constriction of the Cwm Eigiau dam, the high-level part of the line was re-laid in standard gauge (with a deviation to avoid the intermediate incline). The three-pitch gravity incline was straightened and converted to a powered haulage up which building materials were drawn (and on one occasion a full sized locomotive). Later in connection with the building of the Cowlyd dam, a narrow gauge line was built from the head of the main incline, which, together with the line, was retained to assist the maintenance of the dam and the watercourses until the 1980s. The main incline had a further existence as a route for the pipes down to the works and the power station.

Although the aluminium works was eventually served by a rail bridge, none of the grand schemes

to bring a railway to Dolgarrog village and to Trefriw were ever built.

The renaming of Porth Llwyd as Dolgarrog was allegedly to commemorate Y Garrog, a flying dragon that preyed on sheep. Its depredations were ended when a posse of farmers having set a poisoned sheep's carcass as bait, trapped Y Garrog, which they dispatched with their bows and arrows. One Nico Afan refused to take part since a dream predicted that the dragon would kill him, so it was only when the dragon was certified dead did he venture to view the body. In doing so he grazed his leg on the now poisoned corpse causing his immediate demise.

Less hazardous, at Tu Hwnt i'r Afon are the 'Garden Art' themed gardens with sculptures, rare flora and a 2-acre English yew maze, claimed to be the largest in Britain.

10
TAL-Y-BONT and RO-WEN

At Tal-y-bont, the Conwy is joined by the rivers Dulyn and Ro, which having drained the high ground where the population is reckoned not so much as persons per square mile as square miles per person, serve the gentler be-villaged land where the maturing Conway spreads it littoral. The Dulyn arrives at Tal-y-bont via a intriguing near-secret valley where slate speculators gulled the gullible with phantom slate workings that extracted scant rock from the ground but much money from the pockets of the financially naïve.

The Ro takes a more overt route through Ro-wen, once a bustling place with three mills, a fulling pandy and more alehouses than one could shake a stick at. Now it is largely a dormitory clinging jealously to its school, shop and inn with its chief 'industry' being its Youth Hostel. A little way off is Llanbedr-y-Cennin whose name is more poetic than its English translation – St Peter of the leeks, although it is undoubtedly a contraction of the more emotive St Peter of the Daffodils

(*cennin Pedr*). Llanbedr like so many villages has no Post Office, but does have a church, a Salem Independent (Congregational) chapel and a brace of inns.

Along the road is Caerhun Hall, a Tudor house substantially rebuilt in the late 19th century by General Gough of the 10th Hussars when, following distinguished service on the Northwest Frontier, hung up his sword and Sam Browne belt (devised by his boss General Sir Samuel Browne). This house that once presided over the Caerhun Estate is now a conference hotel noted for its garden with a magnificent stand of Cedars of Lebanon. Far older than the Pathan-pursuing general or his house, is the nearby Roman fort of Canovium, extensively excavated in 1929 by Sir Mortimer Wheeler. It is situated near a ford on the river and provided troops marching from Deva (Chester) to Segontium (Caernarfon) with sandal-drying facilities and sustenance, before tackling the stiff climb over Bwlch y Ddeufaen (pass of the two stones) where there are two standing stones that give guidance to travellers on dark and stormy nights.

Situated at the limit of low-water navigation, the fort could be supplied by boat, the nearby remains of a dock, where in more recent centuries many of the sloops that plied the river were built, may well have been where the Romans landed their supplies. Coin finds suggest that the fort may not have been used after the early 2nd century, possibly because more settled times enabled garrisoning of the river crossing to cease.

Located in what had been the northeast corner of the Roman fort is the church of St Mary that has an unusual double bell-cote. As with several other churches in the region there is a notable carved beam, this one showing a female head with flowing hair. The building

appears to date from the 14th century, late in the day for such a foundation. This anomaly has recently been explained by the discovery nearby of traces of what appears to be an earlier church building.

In later times the port hereabouts was Tal-y-cafn, it was overtaken by Trefriw's better facilities, but came into its own again in the 1840s and 1850s when Trefriw was overwhelmed by slate traffic. Until the bridge was built in 1897, a ferry had worked here since at least the beginning of the 14th century, with the Ferry Inn on the western bank dealing with travellers' voyage-induced thirsts. Its counterpart on the eastern bank being the Tal-y-cafn Hotel, a former coaching inn. At various times the vagaries of the Welsh Licencing Laws caused there to be 'wet' side and 'dry' sides of the river on Sundays, ensuring brisk business both for the pubs and the ferry.

Trees shroud the mound that holds the remains of Tal-y-cafn castle which sentinelled the start of the medieval track over the mountain to Aber, which partly followed the Roman Bwlch y Ddeufaen route. There are many remnants of hut-circles showing that long before the Romans came to Britain, even before Rome itself, there were people wresting an existence from the bare, wind-scorched, mountain soil. Above nearby Ro-wen is a monument from an even earlier age when hunter-gathers gradually creeping northwards in the wake of the retreating ice, created a magnificent burial chamber from the boulders left by the glacier-melt. Unlike other contemporary tombs it has not been totally denuded of its earth cover, its name Maen y Bardd ('*the poet's stone*') can scarcely relate to an occupant of the tomb's as in his (or her) time when basic survival would, one imagines, have taken

precedence over flirtations with the Muse. More probably it recalls some forgotten rhymester who, perhaps in medieval times, perched here to construct his *englynion* (strict metre poems) in solitude. Not far away Pen-y-gaer is crowned by a hill fort, its ruined ramparts defended by *Chevaux de Frise*, short standing stones intended to impede attacking horsemen, reminiscent of the 'Dragons' Teeth' anti-tank defences of WW2.

Also high above the valley on a hillside barren save for stone walling, crouched in the lee of Tal-y-fan are further traces of ancient huts that also may well pre-date the pyramids. At one time this was an important intersection of routes, one of which survives as a cattle drovers' walled track that despite being green underfoot, slashes the bleakness like a medieval motorway. Here near a cluster of tiny slate workings are the 'Halfpenny Fields' where drovers overnighted their beasts.

St Celynnin founded a church here in the 6th century presumably to capture the 'passing trade' potential of this intersection. Celynnin may have been a brother of St Rhychwyn and if so he too would have been of royal blood. Celynnin's wood or wattle and daub structure was replaced in the 12th century by a building that forms the nave of the present Llangelynnin church, which is the highest, remotest, and save for Llanrhychwyn, the oldest church in Wales still in use. The chancel was added later and later again *Capel Meibion* was added to accommodate the men where they could not see the women and thus be spared lustful thoughts (or was it the other way about?) There have been repairs over the centuries, the last major makeover being in 1987. It has a nice reader's desk but only vestiges of the rood loft and gallery. The fact that a gallery was needed testifies to the appreciable numbers prior to the Black Death, survivors of which were forced down to lower levels by the 'global cooling' of the late 14th century. A spring of some kind clearly existed long before the saint's time and undoubtedly accounts for the traces of early occupation and of a fort, all sited more defensibly a little way off at Cerrig y Dinas. This spring is manifest today as the holy well *Ffynnon Celynnin* in a corner of the church enclosure. Neatly walled and once roofed, it is pretty structure and its water was renowned for its curative powers. At the opposite side of the enclosure, which due to altitude is devoid of the obligatory yew-trees, there was once an inn that served many a drover until that profession was overtaken by the railways in the 19th century.

Despite the relocation to the valley floor during of the 14th & 15th centuries, it was not until

1840 that a new church was built there. Paradoxically it failed to outlast the one it replaced and since 1980 has been a sculptor's studio. Also maintaining the artistic credentials of the area is the nearby pottery where Vicky Buxton throws her pots and Phillip Owen fires his enamels. Displaying creativity in a different medium are the interesting and unusual Conwy Water Gardens at Ro-wen that offer fishing amongst otters, ducks and other creatures.

A short distance across the river are Bodnant Gardens, an 80 acre estate originally laid out in the late 19th century by a forebear of Lord Aberconwy who was criticised for his association with Lord Halifax, the late 1930s 'no war at any cost', Foreign Secretary. Whatever the rights and wrongs of their Lordships' views, the gardens that the family handed over to the National Trust are quite outstanding and few would challenge their claim to be the finest domestic gardens in Britain.

11
GLAN CONWY

The dominant feature in this area is the 47 Hectare RSPB Conwy Reserve, developed during the building of the A55 Expressway tunnel as a safe year-round haven for wading birds such as godwit. However it has since attracted lapwings, water rail, egrets, sedge and reed warblers and other varieties, making it the most important of the numerous bird watching sites along the north Wales coast. Almost every kind of indigenous bird has been seen and it is now a regular 'port of call' for many migratory species. Despite the presence of raptors, finches and bunting thrive and 'Star' sightings have included terek and marsh sandpipers, bluethroats and black-headed wagtails. In all, more than 200 varieties of bird have been recorded in 'twitchers'' notebooks. In comparatively few years it has become one of the most significant and species-diverse bird reserves in Britain.

Modern Glan Conwy grew out of Llansanffraid a tiny fishing village that doubled as a 'ferryport'

for the perilous transit of the rip tides and shifting sands of the Conwy estuary. Its founding is attributed to St Ffraid (Bridget) an Irish Princess. It appears her father wished her to marry a man of his choice, but she did she not fancy this particular man and in fact did not fancy men at all. In our more cynical times such inclinations would not automatically be ascribed to holiness but in her day they were; a view reinforced by the fact that whenever she looked after her father's cattle they gave milk thrice daily. Consequently when she fled pursued by her father's posse, which caught up with her at the coast, no one was particularly astonished when the piece of cliff-top turf on which she was standing miraculously detached itself and bore her out to sea.

She ended up in Wales on the banks of the Conwy about a quarter of a mile west of the present church. The piece of turf turned into a rock still called '*Tywarchen Ffraid*' (St Ffraid's Turf) allowing her to step ashore unsoaked and unsullied. She found that due to famine the people living along the Conwy were starving, so she gathered an armful of rushes from the water's edge and threw them into the river where they immediately turned into myriads of little dace which in Welsh are called *brwyniaid* from the Welsh word *brwyn* meaning 'rush'. The people cast out their nets, which were immediately and repeatedly filled with fish. Traditionally *brwyniaid* appear in the river Conwy on

February 1st and thus this day is known as *Gŵyl Ffraid* (St Ffraid's Feast Day).

Llansanffraid surviving as it did on fishing, river-boating and a modicum of agriculture, was never a wealthy place but was allegedly more affluent than Conwy town. It is said that if a traveller tendered a sovereign in payment for a small purchase at Conwy several shillings worth of coin would be beyond its resources, so a messenger had to be sent to Llansanffraid to obtain change. Since Conwy had diverse trades and a harbour of some importance, such impecuniousness seems extraordinary and is said to have been due to a curse placed on Conwy because of its ill treatment of a stranded *môr-forwyn* (mermaid) by the men of the town.

Mermaidic manifestation would have been rare at Llansanffraid since it bordered on the habitat of the *Afanc* an encounter with which a mermaid would have feared as much as any human. Get on the right side of a mermaid and she might well warn of storms and perils and even bring prosperity. There was no right side to the fearsome *Afanc* and tales abound of both men and beasts vanishing from riverbanks leaving vestige of neither hair nor hide. Even in our more enlightened times, there are still some who avoid venturing too close to the water's edge.

Near the river bank at the hamlet of Graig, twice as distantly removed from our time as the good St Ffraid, is Hendre Waelod, a Neolithic Burial Chamber. Although adjacent to Coed Tan yr Allt woods that have a fine viewpoint of the rugged west side of the valley, its situation lacks the grandeur of Capel Garmon but the chamber behind the portal dolmens is impressively large. The

enormous capstone lies slightly askew and seems to await the coming of some mighty pre-Celtic Samson to heave it back into place. Access via the portal is blocked but it is possible to squeeze in from the side, touching the stones with hands separated by 150 generations from the hands that shaped and set them.

Windmills may be postcard-picturesque but are more expensive to build, more costly to maintain and less dependable than water mills. Therefore from medieval times wherever fast-flowing water was found it was eagerly harnessed to grind corn to feed a burgeoning population. Later, fullers, weavers, tanners and forge masters in increasing numbers sought similar streams to drive their machinery. These people were able to outbid millers for prime sites but fortunately due to remoteness and less than abundant water, most corn mills in the Conwy area escaped the industrialists' clutches. One such mill was the fine, now restored, Felin Isaf at nearby Pentrefelin powered by the delightful Nant Garreg Ddu. Not far off in Eglwysbach, the cataracts of Nant y Rhaglaw powered another mill of some importance. The 'bach' of this village's name refers not to the Welsh for small but allegedly derives from Bach ap Carwyd who apparently drove off a marauding winged beast, presumably to Dolgarrog.

In the early 19th century the good villagers paid Robert Roberts of Llanrwst £9.00 to depict the coat of arms of King George III who, despite (or possibly because of) his madness was a popular figure in Wales. Unfortunately Mr Roberts could not 'do lions' so the armorials survive in Eglwysbach church with the unicorn partnered by a dog.

Some distance up river but still within the parish of Eglwysbach is the site of Maenan Abbey where the monks settled when Edward I ejected them from Aberconwy to make space for Conwy Castle. There is a popular perception that monks spent their days chanting, praying, digging the garden in their dressing gowns and selling Indulgences – 'Get out of jail free' cards for the Hereafter. But the fact is that monks were both learned and shrewd, the Cistercian abbeys in particular being powerhouses of education, agriculture and contributed to the industrial development of medieval Britain.

All such abbeys were eventually vandalised by Henry VIII, but for this one it was a 'double whammy' having been looted a century earlier by Henry VIII's equally detestable forebear Henry IV, for having supported Owain Glyndŵr. The monastery lands were 'acquired' by Elizeus Wynne who built a house for himself using the stones of the ruined abbey. That house fell into disrepair, the present house that continues the Maenan Abbey name, now the hotel hub of a caravan park, was built by Lord Newborough, of Glynllifon near Caernarfon in the mid 19th century. The total absence of romantic remains for poets to eulogise and painters to immortalise, make it the least known monastic foundation in Wales.

Nearby is Plas Maenan also an hotel, famously once occupied by Henry Jack the controversial Chairman both of the County Council and of the Aluminium Corporation, owners of the Dolgarrog works. Via this latter post he had by 1923 'hi-Jacked' control of all the passenger-carrying narrow gauge railways in northwest Wales. His dedication to the cause of narrow gauge communication was Jesuitical, but financially flawed and he was ousted from his railway appointments for alleged mismanagement. Bearing the brunt of the criticism that followed the 1925 Dolgarrog dam disaster, he left the area to live in Tunbridge Wells under an assumed name. Whether this latter refuge was chosen as a penance is not known.

12
TOWN and CASTLE

In 1826 Thomas Telford's fine suspension bridge eliminated the trauma of the Conwy town ferry as recorded by Fenton who when crossing in the 1780s received *"most unexampled and savage insolence"* when he complained of a two-hour wait. The bridge also served a secondary purpose as a prototype for the much longer but similarly constructed Menai Bridge. It is now closed to traffic but it affords pedestrians a vista of the Castle and close-up view of Stephenson's 1848 rail bridge that served as a similar 'mock up' for his great Britannia crossing of the Menai Straits. The tollhouse, recently restored by the National Trust, is of the standard Telford pattern, well built and offering a high standard of accommodation that in some measure compensated the gatekeeper for the opprobrium and occasional violence that came with the job. Alongside the two 19th-century bridges is the 1955 road bridge that brought so much traffic into the town, that prior to its being replaced by the tunnel, drivers had the opportunity not only to read the paper but also to do the crossword puzzle in the course of a summertime transit of the town.

Obviously the major feature of Conwy is the castle. Although Caernarfon is more complete and Harlech stands higher, many consider Conwy to be the finest extant example of medieval military architecture and is rightly a World Heritage Site. Like other Edwardian castles it was built on a rock that could not be undermined by besiegers, could dominate a major communications route and could be supplied by sea.

Following the departure of the Romans; Angles, Saxons, Jutes and Vikings had fancied their chances in this part of Wales, but the local lads saw off the lot of them. Normans and Plantagenets met a similar lack of 'welcome in the hillsides', but Edward I having sorted out his rebellious barons

turned his attention to the Welsh. He commissioned Master James of St George to build castles of an unprecedented size and complexity to end the Celtic discourtesies once and for all.

One can imagine James looking at the sketches and sucking his teeth saying – "That'll set you back a few groats, boss". In fact the figure for Conwy was £15,000 (a labourer's wages might be around £3.00 per year!) making it the costliest of all the Edwardian castles. It took 4 years to build, probably not much longer than it would take to take to get planning permission today. The ¾ mile-long town walls that were included in the deal, are among the finest examples of a town enclosure in the Britain. The walls were intended to protect the English

colony that served the castle and filled the many 'job opportunities' that the castle created, resulting in what was very much a 'one industry' town. Welsh people were allowed into the town but had to be out before the gates were closed at curfew, any Welshman caught within the walls after that would be liable to find himself missing some of his bits (e.g. his head). Actually the concept of urban living was totally unknown to most Welsh people. The idea of being forced to live in close company with one's neighbours with nowhere to grow corn or graze even a goat and having to confine the pig to the fireside; must have seemed very strange indeed. It must have been astonishing to find that the emptying of chamber pots out of windows was an acceptable sanitary practice, particularly as monoglot Welsh speakers they would have learned the hard way not to look up when the cry of *Gardez l'eau*! was shouted from above. As indeed would the concept of Curfew (*Couvre feu*) when some jumped-up jack-in-office rang a bell to tell you when to put your fire out.

Excluded permanently from the town were the monks of Aberconwy Abbey. They, together with the tomb of Llywelyn the Great, were 'resettled' at Maenan on the east bank of the river some 8 miles upstream where, with a grant of £40 from King Edward, they had to rebuild all over again. The present St Mary's church occupies the Abbey's erstwhile Conwy site.

The castle was never taken by assault, although Edward spent Christmas 1294 cowering behind its massive walls while a Welsh mob 'demmoed' outside. Owain Glyndŵr's forces briefly

occupied it in 1401 more by guile than by force. During the Civil War, despite the structure being dilapidated and not formally garrisoned, some Royalists held out for three months against desultory Cromwellian attack but by that time the whole concept of a castle as a sustainable stronghold had been 'blown apart' by the invention of gunpowder.

Trade must have developed very closely upon the completion of the castle, since the 14th century Aberconwy House (claimed to be the oldest town house in Wales) was built near the quayside to enable its merchant owner to keep an eye on his affairs. This would, suggest that commerce was already well established.

The gem of the town is the stepped-gabled and gate-housed Plas Mawr built in the 1570s by Robert Wynn of the already influential Wynn family. At the other end of the grandeur spectrum is a house on the quayside that at 9'9" x 6', fails to afford the possibility of swinging even the compactest of cats. It was inhabited until the early 20th century, reputedly by a tall man who could not stand up in it and could only lie down diagonally. It is known as the 'Smallest House in Wales', a title that may well be challenged if modern 'starter homes' get any smaller.

With the decline of the Castle as an economic epicentre, the real business of Conwy became maritime, handling the town's trade and trans-shipping into sea-going vessels goods brought down river in sloops. Nestling under the town walls were four shipyards from where well over 100 vessels were launched, some as large as 300 tons. Daniel Defoe in the 17th century described the harbour as 'noble' comparing it favourably with Chester and Liverpool, suggesting that it was a port of some consequence. However these days the main maritime activity is provided by the big and busy Conway Quays marina. Fishing, particularly mussel fishing continues as the quayside shop and the 'Blue Mussel Monument' (by Graeme Mitcheson) testify, although the traditional gathering by women and children from the shoreline rocks has died out. Pearls are still occasionally found in the mussels, but are too minute to have value. The pearls presented by Sir Richard Wynn to Charles II's bride, Catherine of Breganza to demonstrate his solidarity with the Stuart cause (now part of the Royal crown) would probably have come from fresh water mussels at Llanrwst.

It is difficult to reconcile precious pearls and flourishing trade with alleged civic impoverishment but the 'mermaids curse' legend persists. Accounts differ as to how this poor creature became stranded, some say she was trapped by the ebbing tide others that she had suffered an entanglement in a fisherman's net that might not have been accidental. Either way despite it being common knowledge that a mermaid cannot survive long out of water, her cries for help were ignored – derided even – by onlookers. This callousness may have arisen from mermaids' notorious penchant for luring seamen onto rocky shores causing her to be seen as a creature too dangerous to release, on the other hand her uncommon beauty, the length of her dark tresses and the perfection of her bosom may have, despite obvious physiognomic incompatibilities, given rise to male ambitions of a regrettably concupiscent nature. Anyway for whatever reason, there was no move to restore her to her natural habitat and she suffered a long lingering death. Before she perished she cursed the inhabitants of Conwy to perpetual poverty. It seems that this pecuniary penalty did eventually expire, but it was replaced by other strictures, the Town Hall allegedly built on the very spot where the mermaid died, inexplicably burned down in 1966 and even its replacement also caught fire. At the time of this second conflagration many worthy citizens heard the mermaid's laugh echoing through the town. Since to date no other attributable disasters have occurred it is hoped that the wrong is now finally expiated.

It was of course Telford's bridge that brought the coach traffic to the town, with the Castle Hotel offering sustenance and a change of horses as well as accommodation for those long-pocketed and unhurried travellers who preferred not to travel by night. Those coming from Chester would have had a tedious but uneventful journey, but on continuing west to Bangor would soon become aware that the river was a geological frontier and that henceforth their onward journey would generate some nasty surprises.

13
DEGANWY and LLANDUDNO JUNCTION

The name Llandudno Junction has railway connotations but now big interchanges on the A55 make it more redolent of Spaghetti Junction. It is from here that the Expressway dives underground like a startled stoat into a tunnel that is not a tunnel at all but a series of concrete boxes buried in the estuary bed. Cars and lorries intent on Holyhead, rush through it heedless of the fact that should the anchorages fail the whole ½ mile of it would invoke Archimedes principle and rise to snake across the surface like some monstrous sea serpent. Whilst this underpass enables Conwy Morfa to be reached from the Junction in as many minutes as it once took hours, its users are denied the view of Conwy Castle that only the dawdling or those of a claustrophobic inclination now enjoy. The casting of the sections of the tunnel in the late 1980s stirred old memories of the concrete components of the Mulberry Harbour, on which the success of D-Day depended, being built just across the water from Deganwy, over 40 years before.

In truth Llandudno Junction is a misnomer and by rights should be Llandudno Junctions since not only are trains diverted north to the seaside delights of Llandudno itself, but also south to the erstwhile slateopolis of Blaenau Ffestiniog. It is one of the few double-junctions to survive into the 21st century and the recycling of slate tips may remove the Damoclean axe that has been poised over the Blaenau line since Dr Beeching first wielded it. More than a village but less than a town, it lacks any mysterious past that excites interest both in locations and in women. Originally it was the little fishing and ferrying hamlet of Tremarl, a trifling corner of the ancient parish of Llangwstennin, but the area was not short of skills as the bronze axe-head found at Bryn Pydew testifies. These skills were applied to support Conwy shipbuilding and very much so to railway service, the major locomotive depot being the pride of the London and North Western Railway and the envy of every other railway. Happily the depot's official designation 6G is perpetuated as a road name.

The railway-developed skills attracted other industries, most now sadly vanished, including the Colloidal Slate Works sited during the 1930s equidistant from Blaenau and Bethesda whose quarries' fortunes it sought to rejuvenate by painting roofing slates in pretty colours. The chief industry is now an outstation of the Welsh Assembly Government, an organisation whose creators

apparently failed to realise that the dictionary would define its acronym as *A tiresomely humorous person*.

Although outwardly an equally modern settlement, Deganwy is more historically important. It is a townlet dominated by two erotically rounded peaks redolent of some ancient giantess, probably predating any significant occupation on the other side of the river at what we now call Conwy. It is said that the name derives from *Din-gonwy* or *Dinas Ganwy* which would mean 'Fort on the River Conwy', but equally could be a corruption of the early Brythonic name *Decantouion*.

Finds of Samian pottery and early 4th century Constantinian coins confirm a Roman presence on what was an ancient, tribally occupied site, becoming important in the 6th century as the court of Maelgwyn Gwynedd, the most influential figure in pre-Norman Wales. He was reviled as a tyrant but also praised as the patron of Saints Cybi and Seiriol since undeniably in his later years he facilitated the setting up of cells by them and possibly other holy proselytisers.

The settlement was captured and destroyed successively by the Danes and the Vikings prior to being seized by the Normans led by Robert of Rhyddlan who built a castle that was lauded by Giraldus Cambrensis when he passed this way in 1188. Captured by Llywelyn the Great in the 13th century it was destroyed by his son Dafydd to deny it to the English. Henry III partly rebuilt it, his work being the source of much of the modern vestiges. Eventually it was starved out and destroyed by Llywelyn the Great's grandson Llywelyn ap Gruffudd, after which the English gave up trying to

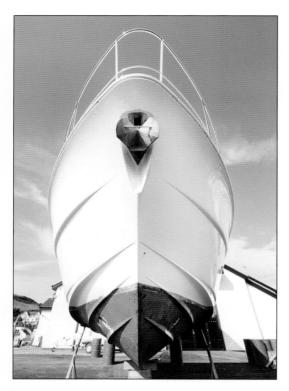

establish any kind of presence here. So when Henry's son Edward I built a castle it was on a much more defensible site across the estuary at Conwy with sea access that made it virtually siege-proof. His contractor, Master James reputedly was able to cut his costs by 'recycling' stones from the ruins at Deganwy, hence the dearth of remains.

In the mid-19th century the railways that had robbed Conwy of its maritime trade brought a new prosperity to Deganwy. The London & North Western Railway's Caernarfon to Llanberis branch enabled half a score of quarries to burgeon, producing a cornucopia of slate that would have overwhelmed the already overstretched Caernarfon quays. Porthmadog could be reached via Afonwen but its quaysides were was not readily accessible by standard gauge and anyway they were at bursting point from Blaenau traffic. More importantly, the extension of the Betws-y-coed line to reach the riches of Blaenau Ffestiniog, was the railway company's ultimate objective. Therefore they built a new, slate-dedicated dock at Deganwy reached from their Llandudno branch. Thus quarry wagons, filled high on distant mountains, could be carried on transporter trucks right up to the waiting vessels. Although this dock had to wait for the 'Marina Era' to achieve its full potential, in the early1870s it was one of the busiest slate ports in Britain.

At Bryniau to the north are the ruins of a tower. As tends to be everything that reaches back much beyond human memory, it has been wrongly described as Roman. Whilst its date and purpose is uncertain, since the castle had only a restricted seaward view it is thought to be an 'early warning system' to alert Conwy castle of vessels approaching with unfriendly intent.

Llangwstennin, which is moated by marsh and urbanly imprisoned by Colwyn, Llandudno, Deganwy and Llandudno Junction, contrives to maintain a whiff of rurality. The parochial dedication comes from St Cystennin who, with his brother St Peblig and mother St Helen, brought the Celtic form of monasticism from Gaul. Secularly, the adjacent area is Mochdre, (Pig Town) a name that presumably has agricultural associations but just possibly could derive from the Mabonigion tale of a theft of pigs from south Wales, which caused frightful mayhem at the time. In the 19th century Mochdre achieved fame in railway circles by having the first between-rails water

trough in the world, enabling the Irish Mail to replenish its tender as it thundered non-stop to Holyhead. These days the number of industrial diamonds manufacturers make it renowned as the 'Amsterdam of Wales'.

Presiding over the whole Deganwy area is Gloddaeth, home (or one of the homes) of the Mostyn family who by marriage and some rather challengeable land grabbing, owned much of the area. Built in the 16th century, the house as fine as any in north Wales is now a school.

What the Mostyns did not own round here belonged to the Wynns, their house in this locality being Bodysgallen. Although not on the scale of Bodnant, its gardens are a showpiece. Now a hotel, the building's name allegedly connects it to Caswallen, a 5th century Gwynedd chieftain, but it is more probable that the name derives from *ysgallen*, (thistles).

14
LLANDUDNO

Standing as it does on a neck of the Creuddyn peninsular, Llandudno is a most confusing town. Gloddaeth Avenue has a sea front at each end, the lifeboat station is sited just about as far from the sea as it is possible to get, and there are two golf clubs so close together that a careless hook could almost land you on the right green but the wrong course.

It is not easy standing among the iron-canopied shopping parades or the sea-front sweep of grand hotels of this purpose-built resort, to realise that this was a mining town with mines that are older than King Solomon's and predate by a thousand years the siege of Troy. Surrounded by fine Victorian architecture it is hard to appreciate that this has been a settlement for almost forty centuries.

It is possible that the next person you pass in the street had a grandfather (prefixed with anything up to 150 greats) who won copper ore from deep within the Great Orme, (*Penygogarth*) and lived in

a hut whose circle might be traced on the mass of limestone that overshadows the town like a great monolith but in reality, thanks to the work of millennia of miners, is as hollow as a politician's promise.

The name Orme is said to derive from a Viking word for serpent that to those approaching from the sea it must have resembled. The Vikings proved an even bigger menace than the Saxons and other assorted scallywags had been. However in a great sea battle in 856 off Morfa Rhiannedd (North Shore), Rhodri Mawr made it clear to the Norse invaders or such few as survived, that round here was a Zero Tolerance Zone for pillage and rape and that in future they should try their luck elsewhere.

Older than the Vikings, older even than the mining is Llety'r Filiast, ('*the lair of the greyhound bitch*') a much-ruined chambered tomb situated close to the summit of Great Orme where one can 'see forever' or at least as far as the Isle of Man, Cumbria and the Wicklow peaks. Here the ex-lighthouse, ex-telegraph, ex-radar station, restaurant welcomes visitors and nearby is Bishop's quarry, a limestone excavation whose name perpetuates the gifting of the Manor of Gogarth to Bishop Anian of

Bangor by the Normans to reward his acquiescence in accepting the authority of Rome.

This summit can be effortlessly reached by a two-stage funicular tramway, the upper pitch being a fairly ordinary two-car counterbalanced arrangement on a reserved track, but the lower pitch uniquely traverses steep streets. This somewhat anachronistic tramway is now supplemented by a more adventurous overhead chairlift.

Even more adventurous was the first ascent of the Great Orme by motorcar in 1911 by Beatrice Blore-Browne in a 10 hp Singer, this feat being trumped by her husband George Browne when he in 1920 drove up Snowdon in a 14 hp Angus Sanderson. The redoubtable lady who sadly died in her early 30s is commemorated by the epitaph *She feared naught but God* on a unique 'Winged Wheel' monument in St Tudno's churchyard.

St Tudno was one of the seven sons of King Seithenyn whose legendary kingdom in Cardigan Bay was inundated, apparently due to Seithenyn's attention being directed towards the ladies rather than the sea defences of his realm. To prepare himself for a life of good works in propitiation for his father's neglectful loss of real estate, Tudno studied in St Dunawd's college at Bangor on Dee, before 'setting up shop' in Ogof Llech ('*slab cave*'), just below the Orme-encircling Marine Drive. This now near-inaccessible cavern, once readily reached from the sea, is elaborately lined with sandstone to form an octagonal chamber with stone seats and a table.

Tales abound, and it has been suggested that it has associations with the Templar Knights of Ysbyty Ifan and also that it was once used by German prisoners of war attempting to escape by submarine. Actually the masonry seems to date from its 17th century use as a fishing lodge by the Mostyn family.

By the time this masonry was installed Tudno had long gone having built his church near the Orme's summit. His structure was replaced in the 12th century by a building that was destroyed in the great storm of 1839. It was restored preserving some of the old features such as a carved wooden roof boss depicting the 'stigmata' or five wounds of Christ, an almost unique survivor of an emblem once common in Wales. There is also an ancient beam with a carved serpent upon it echoing the similar feature at Dolwyddelan.

The Orme's ores were not smelted here, hence Llandudno never became a smokestack town, but it nearly became a sea port, since in the mid-19th century the Mostyn Estate proposed a dock on North Shore to ship coal from its Flintshire collieries, in the event it was decided instead to create a genteel resort. A jetty was built with commerce in mind, but when the railway began to bring in trippers in numbers measured in trainloads rather than headcount, this was soon converted into the longest and most splendid pleasure pier in Wales. Before it was burnt down, a pavilion having storey piled on storey in mock Maharajan style made the pier a diadem for this 'Queen of Resorts' whose motto *Hardd, Hafan, Hedd* ('beautiful haven of peace') was inspired by the Queen of Roumania, a one-time visitor.

The Great Orme is counterpointed by the Little Orme; although the latter is but a poor reflection, it does have a claim to fame in that during Elizabethan times when 'no popery' was the buzzword, Robert Pugh of Penrhyn Hall and William Davies a Catholic priest assembled a secret press in one of the sea-facing caves, printing banned material including a small book *The Christian Mirror*, the earliest instance of publishing in Wales. Arrested, Pugh was able to invoke the 'Old Boy' network but Davies was gruesomely put to death, amends being made 300 years later when he was canonised as a saint.

Whilst one must now bathe without the modesty of a bathing machine and Signor Ferrari no longer

displays his performing fleas; donkeys may still be ridden although the adventurous may find kite surfing, kite buggying, kite boarding and dry skiing more to their taste.

If the town's famous son is 'Billy' Hughes who became Prime Minister of Australia, its most famous daughter must be Alice Lidell of Wonderland fame who is celebrated by the Wonderland Centre. Alice's father Dean Lidell built a holiday home for his family on West Shore that became the lately demolished Gogarth Abbey Hotel. Adjacent there is memorial to the White Rabbit, but alas the account it bears that the Reverend Dodgson (Lewis Caroll) gained inspiration amongst the bunnies of the Great Orme may be fiction.

Llandudno has what is irreverently called 'Jack the Ripper's' church. St Paul's church attracted this scurrilous sobriquet through being built in memory of the Duke of Clarence, Queen Victoria's son who was at one time alleged to be responsible for the notorious 19th century Whitechapel Murders.

There are a number of non-conformist chapels, many being ornate structures commissioned by wealthy incomers, but Tabernacl Baptist Church claims precedence from being an 18th century foundation by some of the earliest 'Dissenting' worshipers in the town. This chapel drew further kudos in 1936 when its pastor the Reverend Lewis Valentine became a folk hero by being one of the three arsonists who symbolically set fire to an RAF hut at Penrhos near Pwllheli. Earlier the Baptists had gained notoriety rather than fame when in 1847 all but three of the congregation were ejected for plundering a wrecked ship. Even so they attracted less opprobrium than did the Wesleyans whose entire membership was debarred for the same reason. The Presbyterians smugly claimed that a mere two of their flock suffered exclusion.

Despite the fall from favour of the 'Seaside Holiday', Llandudno, bolstered by the Conference Trade and the 'Short Break', continues to flourish and despite no longer being the 'Resort of Queens' still reigns as the 'Queen of Resorts'.

15
THE COAST

Bangor-bound travellers leaving Conwy by the North Gate were almost immediately faced with the rounding of Penmaenbach Headland, fortunately this 'To Hell in a Handcart' negotiation was reduced from the terrifying to the mere frightening by the 1820s road works, but even taking this improved route was unwise when winter storms and reaching waves threatened to snatch coaches from the exiguous carriageway and immolate their passengers on the rocks below. The alternative was to make the extremely daunting ascent of the Sychnant Pass, probably walking behind or even pushing one's coach, only to face the risk of a runaway down the other side bringing about a precipitate arrival at Dwygyfylchi.

To today's speeding motorist Dwygyfylchi is a mere between-tunnels corner-of-the-eye glimpse, yet for those refusing to be hurried a diversion via the Sychnant Pass will delight the senses. Well-pursed Victorians appreciated its ambience and built retirement homes such as tree-sheltered

Pensychnant, now a nature reserve. Today, Pensychnant works zelously with local and national wildlife and conservation organisations to foster the public's appreciation of nature and to safeguard and record the wildlife and natural beauty of North Wales. There certainly is plenty of it to safeguard and record – buzzards, hawks, kestrels, herons and for those that would venture here at dusk, owls and bats. Everywhere horses and the ubiquitous Snowdon goats run wild. Equally notable is Pendyffryn Hall once occcupied by the Darbishires of Penmaenmawr quarry who were great benefactors to the whole area.

Building over the last couple of hundred years has made Dwygyfylchi a larger but quieter place than when the hamlets of Isa-pen and Ucha-pen first coalesced into a mining village. At one time a variety of minerals such as copper ore, manganese, pyrites and feldspar were won, but only the copper working continued into the 19th century. It had the obligatory two chapels (one to go to, one never to set foot in) as well as the church dedicated to Gwynin a rather shadowy 7th century saint of the type mistrusted by the Normans, said to be the son of a wicked prince named Helyg. The present church opened in 1889 replaced a 17th century building which in its turn replaced a 16th century church, some of whose timbers are incorporated in the present structure. The name of the settlement of Capelulo may suggest a foundation by the apocryphal St Ulo.

The high ground abounds with barrows, cromlechs, standing stones, ancient encampments, fortresses, house-platforms and hut circles, testifying to a multi-millennia history of occupation. The name of one upright stone Maen y Campau, suggests 'games', probably literary and musical contests (Eisteddfodau) rather than athletic activities.

The ancient traveller might have been able to avoid the Penmaenbach headland but no such cop-out was available at the equally discouraging Penmaenmawr Point where every turn of the coach's wheels could have brought calamity, particularly if the coachman had steeled himself with liberal libations. Fortunately tunnelling has robbed all promontories of peril and now the main threats to motorists are speed cameras.

From Conwy Mountain (*Mynydd y Dref*) right along the north of the Llŷn Peninsular, the high coastal bluffs are a rich source of granite. It was worked at Penmaenbach but the hardest and most prized rock is at Penmaenmawr and although its flanking workings of Graiglwyd and

Llanfairfechan are now mere industrial archaeological sites abounding in fauna and flora, the main Penmaenmawr quarry is very much in business. It was opened in the 1830s as a source of setts, laboriously hand-fashioned on site to surface countless Coronation Streets all over the north of England. With such streets no longer pounded by iron-shod hooves and iron-tyred wheels, the quarry has turned to road-stone aggregates in such prodigious quantities that the Ordnance Survey has to revise downwards the spot heights on each successive map edition. Material used to be moved by an extensive internal rail network (both standard & 3' gauge) and gravity inclines into huge hoppers to load onto ships at the jetties or into rail wagons, but now all movement is by belt-conveyors or trucks. The huge quarry clock (The Big Ben of Wales) was a gift by the Euclid Company of America to mark the beginning of the phasing out of internal rail transport and its replacement by Euclid trucks. Actually there was a marked overlap of transport technology, this quarry having been an early user of giant road-vehicles became one of the last users of De Winton 'Coffee Pot' locomotives. In fact Mr R. C. Darbishire had a 2' gauge replica of a De Winton made in the quarry workshops for a railway in the garden of his Plas Mawr house.

Regrettably quarrying has over decades obliterated Braich y Dinas, an Iron Age hill fort. Again like the high ground inland there is evidence of occupation in milder-climated times, such as the 'Druid's Circle', where despite having no association with druids, neo -druidic ceremonies are

occasionally still carried out although it seems that the sacrifice of virgins is no longer included in the rites.

At Cwm Graiglwyd, there was a major Neolithic axe-head factory, the same agate-hard, quartz-free Diorite stone, that now delights highway engineers, being apparently equally ideal for the immolation of enemies, the dispatch of evil beasties or the chopping of firewood. This 4th millennium B.C. axe manufacture was presumably Wales' first export business, shipping to other parts of Britain and probably to Europe as well. This may indicate that even at this early time, there existed in Wales some kind of currency-based economy.

The villages of Penmaenmawr and Llanfairfechan were each a peculiar mixture, part quarrying community, part top-of-the-market holiday resort. The size of quarry workers' homes reflected their work-place status with the Ruabon brick-embellished homes of the clerks and supervisors subtly sited in streets unsullied by the dusty boots of the manual grades who dwelt in more modest terraces. As regards visitors, those who stayed at Llandudno's smart hotels considered themselves superior to the Colwyn Bay crowd and certainly much above the Rhyl rabble, but those that holidayed at Penmaenmawr and Llanfairfechan considered themselves 'top of the tree', (or as the local people would say – *crachach*). Such folk,

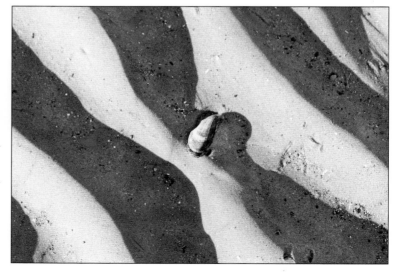

successful Lancashire mill owners or Manchester merchants, who had made 'a bit of brass', did not stay in hotels, but 'took a house' from amongst the large properties specially built for summer lets. The family would be accompanied by a retinue of servants, dogs, cats etc, in a total transhumanance reminiscent of graziers' spring and autumn movement between *hendre* and *hafod*. The household would stay

for months but except for perhaps August, the breadwinner would only be there at weekends. Lesser folk might take a set of rooms or even stay in a boarding house, but they would find that landladies preferred to maintain a selected clientele so that the gentry would be spared mingling with the hoi polloi when they took their morning constitutional on the promenade. So fashionable did the area become that it also attracted national figures, Gladstone for instance coming to Penmaenmawr almost every summer during his later years, during which time he sponsored the building of St Seiriol's church.

St Seiriol the Fair, so called because of his lack of pigmentation rather than perceived even-handedness, established Penmon Priory on Anglesey. He is thought to have at one time established a cell at Graiglwyd. A 20th century lustre was added to his name

when the SS St Seiriol took part in the Dunkirk evacuation.

A more modern divine was Cynan aka Sir Cynan Evans-Jones knighted for services to the cultural life of Wales and the only Welsh poet to be twice elected as Archdruid, ministered at Penmaenmawr during the 1920s. One of his poems paid tribute to Colonel Darbishire of the quarry family.

List of Photographs

Acknowledgements

This third book on the rivers of North Wales has taken nearly three years for Jean to explore the vast area covered by the Conwy and its main tributaries and Alun to research and write the text. As with the other books, without the assistance of many people contributing information and suggestions for little-known places to explore, it would be much the poorer.

Jean has appreciated the intrepid people who have accompanied her on explorations helping to carry kit and offering hospitality. Alun, once again, has appreciated endless assistance and information. As with the other two books, both have made many new friends.

Dan Amor – Llanrwst Almshouses
Jock Andrews
Prifardd Myrddin ap Dafydd
Ascend Rope Access Specialists
Rev Tom Bonnet – St Mary Caerhun
Bryncrug Readers Group
Gill & Mick Bucknall – Pickwicks
Vicky Buxton & Philip Owen
Norman Cade – Felin Isaf
CADW
Barbara Carter
Colin Cartwright – Conwy Valley Railway Museum
David Chapman – Ancient Arts
Linda Clare
Cobdens Hotel
Jeff & Betsan Collin – Snowdonia Antiques
Netti Collister
Del & Sally Davies
Lady Alice Douglas
Nuala Dunn
Will Edwards – Tŷ Mawr
Twm Elias
Nerys Ellis – Hafod Ifan
Y Parch Eirlys Gruffydd
Ken Gruffydd
Tony Hammond – Great Orme Mines
Ann Harrison – Conwy Water Gardens
Rev Clive Hillman – St Tudclud
Heather Hughes – Cwmanog Isaf Farm
Rachel A Jacobson
Giovanni Jacovelli – Garden Art
Brian & Mary Janering
Bill Jones MBE
Bob Jones – Trefriw Quay

Ela Jones – Cwlwm – Y Felin
Griff R Jones (RIP)
Rowland Jones
Trevor Jones & Martin Parry – Conwy Mussels
Llyn Conwy Fly Fishing Club
Tim & Ayla Maddox – Tu Hwnt i'r Bont
Andy McLauchlin
David Mortimer-Jones – Tyddyn Cynal
Jenny & Miles Moulding
The National Trust
Sheila & Terry Potter
Rev Martin Riley
David Roberts – Kaplan-Caerhun Hall
Hilary Rodgers-Jones – Trefriw Wells Spa
Kathy Roper
Pat Rowley
RSPB Conwy
Carole Shearman
George Smith – Outreach Rescue
Angela & Bill Swann
Mair Thomas
Julian Thompson – Pensychnant
Efstathios Tsirmpas
Anita & Seth Walmsley
Peter Welford – Gwydir Castle
Ann Williams – Tŷ Gobaith Hospice
Bryn & Sue Williams – Gwern Gof Uchaf
David & Elizabeth Williams – Gwern Gof
Elaine & Morgan Williams – Trefriw Mill
Euros & Sian Williams – Cilcennus Fferm
Michael & Tracy Williams
Wilfred Williams
Robert White – Cae Coch
Jane Whittle
Oliver & Rebecca Yates

A very special thanks to:
Chris Terrell for the excellent maps
Iolo Williams for the Foreword
Gruff Ellis for his special knowledge of the Upper Conwy

By the same authors, by the same press:

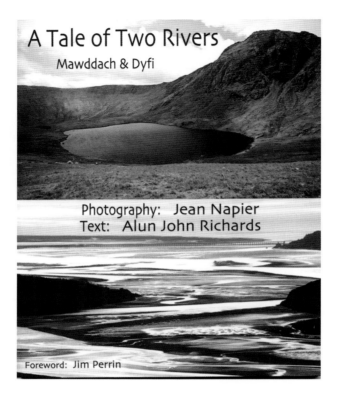

A TALE OF TWO RIVERS

MAWDDACH & DYFI

Alun Richards' myths and legends accompany Jean Napier's evocative images in a journey
through time and distance, from source to sea, of these two great rivers of Wales.
128 pages
£12.00

Published by Gwasg Carreg Gwlach
12 Iard yr Orsaf, Llanrwst, Conwy, Wales LL26 0EH
Tel 01492 642031 Fax 01492 641502
e-mail: llyfrau@carreg-gwalch.com
www.carreg-gwalch.com

By the same authors, by the same press:

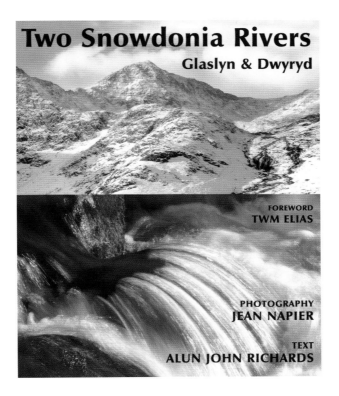

Two Snowdonia Rivers
Glaslyn & Dwyryd

FOREWORD
TWM ELIAS

PHOTOGRAPHY
JEAN NAPIER

TEXT
ALUN JOHN RICHARDS

TWO SNOWDONIA RIVERS

GLASLYN & DWYRYD

Jean Napier's images and Alun Richards' text add layer upon layer of insight into the wealth of heritage and stunning beauty of this magical part of Snowdonia. The rich mix of tales, history and imagery brings alive the landscape we love so much.

144 pages

£12.00

Published by Gwasg Carreg Gwlach
12 Iard yr Orsaf, Llanrwst, Conwy, Wales LL26 0EH
Tel 01492 642031 Fax 01492 641502
e-mail: llyfrau@carreg-gwalch.com
www.carreg-gwalch.com